COACHING
SKILLS
for Riding Teachers

COACHING SKILLS
for Riding Teachers

ISLAY AUTY
BA, FBHS

KENILWORTH PRESS

PICTURE CREDITS

Illustrations and line drawings – Dianne Breeze.
Photos – PSV: cover and p155; Shaw-Shot: pp36, 42, 83, 126.
Cover photo: Sienna Myson Davies riding Welton Jazz at the
European Pony Championships in Saumur, France, July 2006.

First published in the UK by
Kenilworth Press, an imprint of Quiller Publishing Ltd

British Library Cataloguing in Publication Data
A catalogue record for this book is available from the British Library

ISBN 978-1-905693-08-5

Printed in Malta by Gutenberg Press
Book design by Sharyn Troughton

Disclaimer of Liability
The author and publisher shall have neither liability nor responsibility to any person or
entity with respect to any loss or damage caused or alleged to be caused directly or
indirectly by the information contained in this book. While the book is as accurate as the
author can make it, there may be errors, omissions and inaccuracies.

KENILWORTH PRESS

An imprint of Quiller Publishing Ltd
Wykey House, Wykey, Shrewsbury, SY4 1JA
tel: 01939 261616 fax: 01939 261606
e-mail: info@quillerbooks.com
website: www.kenilworthpress.co.uk

CONTENTS

INTRODUCTION

TO BECOME A RIDING INSTRUCTOR WAS MY DREAM. IT IS A CAREER THAT HAS GIVEN AND CONTINUES TO GIVE ME A FANTASTIC RANGE OF 'HIGHS AND LOWS'.

Let me ask you the following questions:

- What are the challenges of this essentially vocational occupation?

- Where did you start and where can it lead you?

- Where would you like to be in the future?

- Do you consider yourself to be a teacher or a coach and is there a difference?

- Are we still instructors?

- Does the word 'trainer' mean something too?

- Should we specialise in one discipline and if so at what stage of our career?

This book is intended to motivate and inspire you: it will help you to direct your own future and encourage you to 'follow your dream'. It will encourage you to question what you do and how you can do it better. Through your own self-development, your pupils and horses will benefit and you will realise increased job satisfaction.

I took the first step towards becoming a professional riding instructor at the age of nineteen and since then have worked full time in the horse industry. I have taught privately, for Riding Clubs and Pony Clubs, run a riding school for twenty years and more recently trained riders both in the UK and extensively abroad. I have taught children and adults, groups and individuals, nervous riders, competitive riders, career students and anyone and everyone who wanted to improve their expertise on a horse (and some who didn't!). Along the way I have learnt from some of the best people in the horse world. I have developed my skills as an instructor and coach through hard work, commitment to always wanting to be better than I was yesterday and learning from experience. I have seen teaching methods change and develop in the time that I have been involved in this career. Most of what I have learnt has been hugely beneficial to my own development and I am now anxious to share it with you. I hope that you will find some satisfaction in taking from this book anything which may help your own quest for self-development.

How to use this book

I am assuming that, when purchasing this book, you already have some teaching experience and are looking to improve your skills. Even if you have already attained some qualifications as a riding instructor or coach you should still find much to benefit you in reading this book. Through the chapters, I will be challenging you to 'think for yourself' and to 'find the answers', both in this book and through other sources, which may include your day-to-day teaching, observing other instructors and further research within other literature.

Personal development is about setting yourself new goals, seeking to improve your skill and expertise and striving constantly to be 'better today than you were yesterday'. You will find many questions through the book that appear to have no immediate answers. The answers *will be there*, but require you to seek them out by consideration of what the question is asking and then dipping into the relevant chapter to find what you are looking for.

Referring back to the first seven questions I itemised early in the Introduction, I hope that the answers to most of these questions will have been covered, or at least touched on, before you have got very far into this book.

As stated, the book will ask many questions, because my aim is to encourage you to think about your own practice. I want you to consider what is 'good practice' and to stimulate your desire to question what you do and whether and how you can improve it or do it better.

It is never possible to stand still in this world; the passing of time always brings change. Although, by nature, we often feel comfortable with familiarity and consistency, change can be motivating, stimulating and exciting – especially if it brings with it a feeling of greater achievement and success. With that in mind I challenge you to seek to be a better instructor every time you go out to help your pupil(s) and enjoy the satisfaction that their progress and success will give you.

A few definitions

So that, for the rest of the book, I can eliminate the need to duplicate the terms instructor/teacher/coach/trainer in every instance, let us consider briefly the meaning of these terms. (Definitions given are based on those from Chamber's Dictionary.)

Traditionally, riding 'instructors' came from a military background. Modern equestrian sport originated largely from cavalry activities and in fact civilian riders were, at one time, debarred from representing their country in certain of the competition disciplines.

Times have changed, and current definitions relating to 'instructor' include:

Instructor: a teacher or college lecturer.

Instruction: the art of instructing or teaching.

Instruct: to prepare, to inform, to teach.

The British Horse Society Instructor qualifications (BHSAI/BHSII/BHSI) are internationally recognised as quality standards of riding teachers. Definitions relating to 'teacher' and 'coach' and 'trainer' include:

Teacher: one whose profession is, or whose talent is, the ability to impart knowledge, practical skill or understanding.

To teach: to show, to direct, to impart the knowledge or art of, to guide the studies of.

A coach: a private tutor; a professional trainer for athletics, etc.

To coach: to tutor, instruct, prepare for examination.

Train: to prepare for performance by instruction, to instruct and discipline.

Team sports and athletics have traditionally developed with their trainers being called coaches. With the development of organisations such as Sports Coach UK (www.sportscoachuk.org), which has made great strides in bringing together all sports under one umbrella, and the current initiative of the UKCC (United Kingdom Coaching Certificate), trainers in sport are looking more towards having one term which relates to teachers/trainers in all sport. However, old habits die hard and inevitably it will be some time before all 'teachers' in sport call themselves 'coaches'. Logically, so long as an 'instructor' qualification exists then most holders of the qualification will presumably continue to call themselves instructors; with the gradual development of the UK Coaching Certificate, holders will more easily call themselves coaches.

My personal interpretation of these terms to date is that when I have been introducing beginner riders or novices to the early stages of the sport, they have come with limited or no prior knowledge. These people need total information: they need to be *'taught'* exactly what to do and how to do it. This is *'teaching'*, in most cases a new skill. When working with more experienced riders, who already have some ability through past experience, you are not teaching new skills, you are enhancing an already existing ability – you introduce ideas to refine an already present expertise. This is *'coaching'*. In my day-to-day work as a riding instructor (that's what my passport describes as my occupation!) I sometimes teach new skills and coach existing expertise in many situations as well. If you, on the other hand, call yourself a trainer then please continue to feel comfortable with this term also.

For the purposes of this book – which is about 'coaching' – I will favour the term 'coach' throughout, except in those contexts where another term is more appropriate.

I would like to end this discussion about definitions by making an important point. While I believe that, in the future, all teachers in sport will call themselves coaches, for the time being I do not believe it makes any significant difference what we *call* ourselves; it is the end product of what we *do* and what we *produce* that will always speak for our competence.

'YOU' AS A COACH

AS I STATED IN THE INTRODUCTION, MUCH OF THIS BOOK IS ABOUT 'ASKING QUESTIONS': SOME QUESTIONS THAT HAVE IMMEDIATE ANSWERS, SOME QUESTIONS THAT NEED THINKING ABOUT AND MAYBE 'REFLECTION' — REFLECTION MEANING ATTENTIVE CONSIDERATION, A THOUGHT RESULTING FROM CONTEMPLATION.

Here are two such questions:

- What sort of coach do you want to be?
- What makes a good coach?

Qualities of a coach

To be a coach you need:

- Knowledge of the subject.
- To know 'how to coach' and, in some contexts, 'teach'.

✦ To understand people.

✦ To understand different learning styles.

✦ To understand levels of competence (horse and rider).

✦ A range of techniques and tactics to improve performance.

As a coach you must be able to:

✦ Plan lessons and forward-plan programmes of several lessons.

✦ Facilitate learning and experience.

✦ Solve problems.

✦ Assess.

✦ Explain, observe and analyse.

✦ Encourage questioning and self-awareness.

✦ Give feedback and listen to riders' opinions.

Are you:

✦ Enthusiastic?

✦ Committed?

✦ Caring?

✦ Aware of your riders' needs?

✦ Open-minded?

✦ A friend?

✦ Supportive and trustworthy?

✦ Self-reflective?

Developing as a coach

This is something that probably evolves gradually in your work as a coach. You begin to become more aware of your effect as a coach and then develop a retrospective attitude to your work. Reflection enables you to consider what was successful (in a session or with a pupil) and what could be adapted or avoided in a future lesson.

Business Reply Plus
Licence Number
RRKS-LAYJ-UAAZ

Quiller Publishing Ltd
Wykey House
Wykey
Ruyton XI Towns
SHREWSBURY
SY4 1JA

Quiller Press

SWAN HILL PRESS

THE SPORTSMAN'S PRESS

KENILWORTH PRESS

Thank you for buying this book. If you would like to be kept informed about our forthcoming publications please fill in this card, or email us at admin@quillerbooks.com.

Name: --

Address: -- Email Address: -------------------------- Postcode: ------------

1. In order to assist our editors in determining the type of books our readers require please tick your areas of interest in the spaces below:

    ☐ Dogs & Gundogs   ☐ Deer   ☐ Equestrian   ☐ Falconry   ☐ Food & Drink
    ☐ Guns & Shooting   ☐ Fishing   ☐ Field Sports   ☐ Humour   ☐ Wildlife Art

    Are you interested in any subject area not covered above? Please specify ---

2. In which book did you find this card? Please specify title --

3. How did this book come to your notice?

    ☐ Magazine advertisement. Which magazine? ---
    ☐ Book review. Which publication? --
    ☐ In a bookshop. Which bookshop? --
    ☐ Our www.countrybooksdirect.com website.
    ☐ Other internet site. Which site? ---

Visit our website at www.countrybooksdirect.com

Telephone: 01939 261616 • Fax: 01939 261606 • Email: admin@quillerbooks.com

Consider:
  ✦ What worked.
  ✦ Why it worked.
  ✦ What could have gone better.
  ✦ What you could have changed or done differently for a better result.

Coaching is as much about people as it is about the sport itself. The real aim of coaching is to work in partnership with your pupil(s) to empower them to learn, achieve and have fun. Performance is improved if the following areas are promoted:

✦ Enjoyment.
✦ Achievement.
✦ Understanding.

Studying how people learn and recognising the needs of your pupils usually establishes a much deeper interaction between you and your rider(s), but you must also be able to recognise and understand your own values and principles and how these impact on your own behaviour.

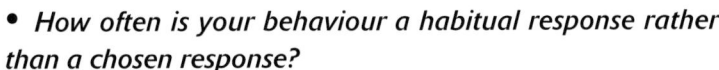

• *How often is your behaviour a habitual response rather than a chosen response?*

As long as you stay open-minded, life in general gives insights and learning that can be applied to coaching. Be able (and willing) to challenge yourself, on a regular basis, on what you are doing and why this is essential to your own development (CPD = Continuous Personal Development).

It is so easy to stay in your comfort zone, but moving out of the status quo and challenging yourself will develop your coaching.

✦   Observe other coaches.
✦   Improve planning, identification of your pupil(s) needs, problem-solving and feedback.
✦   Improve interaction with your pupil(s).

Do you have a role model?

To help your own personal development, identify a successful coach within your sport and ask yourself/find out the following points:

✦   What kind of skills do they have?
✦   Are they a good listener?
✦   How do they coach?
✦   What feedback do they give?
✦   How do they stimulate, motivate and innovate?
✦   How do they review their work?

Also, look at the ways other coaches deal with problems and find solutions.

Other ways to develop your coaching skills

Other ways to develop your skills as a coach could include:

• Never miss an opportunity to talk to others working in a support capacity to riders (physiotherapists, nutritionists, sport psychologists).

• Work with another coach (with whom you have mutual trust and respect) and review each other's sessions and programme. There must be honesty and objectivity between you, with constructive help forthcoming.

• A more experienced coach whom you can use as a mentor can be someone to share problems with and help you to deal with issues and worries. This helps develop your confidence to make choices and find a new way forward.

• Always show confidence and self-control, then you can:

✦ Encourage.

✦ Inspire.

✦ Give confidence. But always be truthful; never give false hope.

● Reflection is fundamental and essential for a coach. And here is an important point to reflect upon:

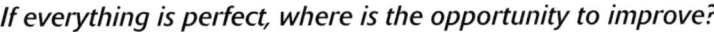

If everything is perfect, where is the opportunity to improve?

● There needs to be a drive that motivates you to be better all the time. This, imparted to your pupils, instils in them an attitude of wanting to analyse and understand what has made a good and not so good performance.

● Often your early experience as a coach is based on what you have learnt as a rider yourself. Aim to improve your own knowledge and understanding of the theory of what you teach.

You learn many skills and become very perceptive during your development as a coach. I reiterate the point that talking with other coaches (in any sport) is INVALUABLE. There is no substitute for experience.

SUMMARY

CHAPTER 1

▨ **CONSIDER YOUR MOTIVATION FOR COACHING.**

▨ **ASK YOURSELF WHAT QUALITIES MAKE A GOOD COACH.**

▨ **THINK ABOUT YOUR ROLE MODEL(S) AND WHY YOU ADMIRE THEM.**

▨ **CONSIDER YOUR OWN SELF-DEVELOPMENT AS A COACH.**

TOP TIPS   TOP TIPS   TOP TIPS   TOP TIPS

■ Show interest in your pupils. They will work with you far more easily if you find out what they feel and are keen to aim for, rather than if you put your own perception on the lesson.

■ If your expectations are not the same as those of your pupils and if you are at cross-purposes one of you will be disappointed. It should **NOT** be your pupil!

■ Work on your own personal development. Never miss an opportunity to learn from other coaches, instructors and trainers to maintain your motivation and enhance your skills.

COMMUNICATION

IN THIS BOOK, COMMUNICATION PRIMARILY MEANS 'TO BE SUCCESSFUL IN CONVEYING ONE'S MEANING OR MESSAGE TO OTHERS; 'TO CONVEY KNOWLEDGE OR INFORMATION'. COMMUNICATION CAN BE CONSIDERED IN THE CONTEXT OF TELEPHONE, MAIL, EMAIL, ROAD, RAIL, AIR OR SEA COMMUNICATION (AS WELL AS OTHER, WIDER CONNOTATIONS RELATING TO HORSE AND RIDER INTERACTION), BUT SINCE THIS BOOK IS ABOUT IMPROVING YOUR COACHING, WE ARE GOING TO CONSIDER COMMUNICATION IN DIRECT PERSON-TO-PERSON TERMS.

First impressions

Appearance

We start to communicate as soon as we meet another person. We communicate initially by our appearance and each person instantly (and often without awareness) begins to form opinions about the other. We may be told not to judge a book by its cover, but we all do so to some degree.

• **When you meet someone for the very first time, what is your first impression of them?**

• **When you know someone well, is your impression of them different from this?**

• **How often have you said: 'When you get to know so and so they are really nice', or: 'You will like so and so when you know her better'?**

The first impression someone has of us may be a lasting one; it may be a good one; it may be less than good. As a coach you will probably want the first impression people form of you to be good – I certainly do.

Dressing for the occasion

In this day and age of 'casual' and 'anything goes', the formality of turnout has largely been lost. Certainly it is considered of less importance than in previous generations.

I wonder what our feeling would be if we saw the Trooping of the Colour parade on the Queen's birthday, or the armed services march past the Cenotaph on Remembrance Sunday, with the ranks of service personnel dressed in cut-off denim jeans, bare-midriff tank tops and trainers? Would we not think that the Prime Minister looked strange if he appeared in the House of Commons in a T-shirt and shorts? We expect a certain standard of appearance from those whom we consider to be in authority or who are leading by example.

If you want to portray an image of value, sincerity and commitment, coupled with authority, knowledge and an air of being in control of the situation, as you should do when presenting yourself to pupils to coach them, then you owe them a personal turnout that is in keeping with the esteem in which you hope they will hold you.

Your turnout should *always* be neat, clean and appropriate for the pupil(s) being taught. Avoid looking as if you have just mucked out twelve horses (even if you have!). Make sure that your boots and jacket are clean and you have given brief consideration to the image you will be putting across. If you are liable to ride a client's horse then make sure you are dressed appropriately. Your insurance may well not be valid if you ride a horse without a hat, and to do this in front of a minor (child under 18) is not setting a good example. What you do on your own horse, in the privacy of your own training situation, is not necessarily what you should be demonstrating as a professional coach, when you are being paid for the service of coaching.

Body language

What information do we give out through the way we 'manage' our body and the space around our body? People generally fall into categories:

- There are the 'touchy feely' types, those who must be in your space. They are tactile, like to hug, kiss, and be close; they are often verbose and engage in much eye contact.

- The exact opposites are the 'don't come too close' sort of people. You get a handshake (if you are lucky); they stay at arm's length and avoid any bodily contact. They do not convey much openness through the face or eyes.

Most of us are somewhere in between these extremes, and again our response will vary according to how well we know the people we are interacting with.

From a coach's point of view, we need to be able to 'read' people. This helps considerably in the way you develop a partnership with them to know what they are like. In particular, when working with children, it is essential to be able to 'read' the parent(s) and from this you will have a much clearer idea of how to teach the child.

The 'vibes' that *you* put out will also help or hinder you. There are many occasions when you may not feel like giving that extra lesson, or perhaps you'd rather go home when the weather is cold and wet. You must try to apply the same amount of commitment and involvement to every lesson, whether it's the first session of the day, or the last lesson of a long weekend of work.

There will be times when you feel irritated and frustrated, perhaps by your lack of achieving the result you were hoping for. In these circumstances try to avoid showing your emotions to your pupil(s) through your body language. An open stance, with hand gestures or movement in your arms, is positive. Crossed arms, hunched shoulders, or head down are all examples of 'negative body language'.

Answering your mobile phone during a lesson does not convey an image of being involved with and interested in your pupil(s)!

Voice

As a coach, your voice is one of your most valuable tools. Use it with care and look after it in the same way that an actor or an opera singer would. Learn to project it without shouting. Breathe well and fully so that you maximise the use of your voice from deep within your chest cavity; don't just 'shout' from the back of your throat.

The biggest threat to your voice is a dusty atmosphere (sadly, many indoor and outdoor schools can wreak havoc with your voice). In exactly the same way that dust will ultimately be damaging to a horse's respiratory system, so it will be to yours. Try to avoid working in dusty conditions, and if you have to, make sure that you drink regular amounts of water throughout the time that you are teaching. Regular intakes of water will help to limit the damaging effect of the dust and keep your vocal cords lubricated.

Consider the weather conditions and avoid 'shouting' against the wind. In windy conditions learn to send your pupil away to work on something and then return to discuss with you the outcome and ongoing work plan. This way you will avoid shouting and not being heard. It's frustrating and distracting for the rider too, if he or she knows you are saying something but is not able to hear.

Listen to your own voice sometimes:

✦   How easy is it to hear?

✦   How much do you repeat a particular phrase or saying?

✦   How much of a 'running commentary' do you keep? (Avoid this!)

✦   How 'easy' are you to listen to?

✦   Does your voice become abrasive/monotonous/irritable/bored?

Be prepared to listen to yourself and to be self-critical – watch a video of yourself teaching from time to time. It can be very revealing. Often your pupils will take a video recording of a lesson you give them. It is quite helpful for your own *reflective practice* to look at it and review your own performance.

How others see you

We've already given some thought to this topic in terms of first impressions and physical appearance, but now I want to look at it in a broader context – adding in the factors of body language and voice which also influence how people perceive one another. I find it fascinating to ask people who don't know me what they have heard about me. If you do this, be prepared to be surprised – shocked even! I have had 'scary', 'bossy', 'frightening', 'opinionated' (I'm certainly the last, but definitely not the first three!).

The point is that, as a coach, you must be aware of how your pupils perceive you. This will change the longer they work with you and the more they get to know you; it will also change as they change. As they become more confident and self-aware they will develop a braver approach to you and any others who may be in authority over them. If the pupil–coach relationship is developing as it should, this is a very natural and desirable situation. Of course, either as they develop, or as you get to know them better (or both) your perceptions of your pupils may also change.

Listening

Listening is a vital part of communication. It is possibly the skill most neglected by many coaches. Coaches are quick to offer information, often instantly and with a great deal of confidence and authority. Their listening skills, however, may be quite inadequate and lacking practice.

Linked to listening is another very important skill which can be a powerful tool for the coach and that is *questioning*. Through first questioning and then listening there are many instances when you can enhance your knowledge of a pupil, particularly with a new rider whom you have not taught before.

• *When you ask a question, do you listen to the answer?*

If you ask a rider a question and then fail to listen to the answer or, worse still, ignore the answer, you will risk alienating your pupil and encouraging a feeling from them that you are not really interested in their contribution. This can be damaging in both the short- and long-term development of the relationship.

Becoming a good listener requires practice! Listening is not just about hearing someone speak. I am sure you can recall occasions when you have said something and the person to whom you have spoken hears you speak but fails to truly listen to what you have said.

Consider some of the following points:

• Listening requires you to concentrate and practise the skill of hearing what someone is saying to you.

• You must allow time to listen and then time to assess and react to what has been said, choosing the appropriate further action.

• Some people are naturally good listeners; they tend to be people who are interested in others and not just absorbed in themselves.

• Body language plays a part in your ability to listen well. Eye contact with the speaker can be helpful (although not always essential if your pupil is speaking to you while on the horse). Nodding and smiling encourage further dialogue. On the other hand, yawning, or eyes roving around the environment signify concentration elsewhere, rather than on the speaker.

• Asking a question which leads the pupil deeper into the subject adds to the pupil's feeling of an engaged listener.

• When listening ensure that you do not have preconceived opinions as to the type of response or information you will receive.

A rider listening to her coach.

You can no doubt recall occasions when you have been speaking and one or more of the following has occurred – the person to whom you are speaking:

✦ Finishes your sentence for you.
✦ Looks past you at someone or something that takes their interest more than your conversation.
✦ Agrees with you or says yes/no, when that response is totally inappropriate.
✦ Starts talking to a third party in the middle of your conversation.
✦ Loses concentration and is distracted by someone or something else in range.

Make sure that in your role as a coach you are never tempted to commit any of these 'sins'.

To improve your skills as a coach you must improve your listening skills. Some of the following points may help, but you must practise them:

- Concentrate – make sure that you can recall the points you have been told.

- Ensure that you are not trying to think of several things at once while attempting to listen.

- Work on your body language, involvement, eye contact (where possible); maintain an inviting, open body language.

- Avoid relating what you are being told to your own experiences, as you will be tempted to tell them about your similar experience and in so doing you stop listening to them.

- Avoid intervening with a joke or a short cut because you are bored with listening.

- Do not agree/disagree with everything said just to avoid listening properly.

- Avoid jumping in to disagree or argue, as this may intimidate your pupil.

- Avoid listening in a judgemental way so that you label the respondent (for example) 'arrogant' or 'lazy' through prejudgement.

- Use questions to clarify information or lead your pupil(s) on further.

- Repeat key points, which will prove you are listening, and consolidate the information. For example: 'So what you said was…' or 'Do you mean …?'

- Thank your pupil(s) for their input.

- Show a sincere interest in your pupil(s).

- *Make* time to listen – it will pay dividends in your coaching.

LISTENING will ensure that you are continually in touch with how your pupils are feeling about the direction of their training.

Questions

Questions and the ensuing answers become hugely valuable tools in developing the relationship between yourself and your pupil(s).

Your riders must develop confidence in your questioning style and then they will begin to realise what an asset questions can be in the communication between the two of you.

It is very easy to take control of a lesson and not allow your pupil(s) to take an active part in how the session evolves. Questions used appropriately and strategically through a lesson will help to avoid this and allow the rider to be actively involved in the way the lesson is directed.

To reiterate the point made in the previous section: *questions become pretty irrelevant unless you are prepared to LISTEN to the answers.* Answers to questions can:

- Give you information about the horse and/or rider.
- Raise awareness.
- Encourage involvement.
- Encourage communication.
- Reveal current knowledge or thinking.
- Encourage focus or concentration.
- Promote thinking and encourage new ideas.
- Encourage critical analysis.
- Confirm understanding.
- Clarify.

✦ Promote concepts of independence and responsibility.

✦ Develop confidence and self-expression.

✦ Add variety to the lesson.

How to ask questions

A question may be 'open' or 'closed'.

Closed questions

• Tend to have 'yes' or 'no' answers, or only one option as an answer. For example: 'Are you tired?' would probably have a 'yes' or 'no' answer.

• Tend to start with *'Are you ...?' 'Do you ...?' 'Have you ...?'*

• Are appropriate to ascertain basic information, to confirm facts, to confirm agreement and to reach decisions when there are only two options.

Consider some of the following closed questions:

How old is your horse?

How long have you been riding?

Have you jumped before?

Do you ever work without your stirrups?

Are you ready to work in canter now?

Open questions

- Invite a broader and more expansive response.

- Encourage personal opinions and experiences.

- Can stimulate a number of possible answers.

- Can help a pupil to feel that the coach is more interested in them.

- Often start with *What, Where, How, Can you tell me, Which, When?*

Open questions can be much more versatile than closed questions in that they may:

1. Encourage reflection.
2. Encourage further questions to reveal greater depth in the answer.
3. Encourage the respondent to concentrate on one aspect of the answer.
4. (In different circumstances from the previous point) lead the respondent onto another subject from the original one questioned.
5. Be hypothetical.

Consider some of the following open questions:

- *Can you tell me* about your horse?

- *How* did you feel when you won that competition?

- *Which* direction did you take when you rode the fence at the top of the hill?

- *When* will you introduce the horse to cross-country fences?

- *What* do you do when you feel yourself get anxious?

Any of the above questions could invite subsequent questions, which could be asked depending on the initial response.

Questions are probably one of your most powerful tools in your coaching 'tool box'.

How you use questions is also crucial to the way they are perceived by the pupil. As your coaching experience develops, your questioning skills become more competent and the questions that you ask begin to come more readily and be more appropriate to each situation.

Make sure that your questions are asked in a friendly way and never in a manner that could make the pupil feel defensive towards you. If questions are well thought out and posed (one at a time) they can encourage rapport with your pupil and put them at ease with you.

Other categories of questions

In addition to being closed or open, questions can be categorised as follows:

- *Leading questions:* these focus the answer into a specific area of discussion. For example: 'What are the aids for shoulder-in?'

- *Follow-on questions:* these can narrow the focus on the subject or probe more deeply into the subject to determine the depth of knowledge. For example: 'Could you talk about the angle of the horse in shoulder-in?' 'What value does shoulder-in have for the horse's development?'

- *Reflective questions:* these encourage the pupil to rethink what they may have said, for clarification. They enable you to add information to enhance the understanding. For example: 'So am I to understand that you think shoulder-in encourages the horse to take more weight on the hind legs?'

- *Hypothetical questions:* these can encourage a pupil to consider an alternative answer and may be useful to ensure clarity of the subject. For example: 'So if you rode the shoulder-in with too much angle, what would happen then?'

Remember that the success of questioning lies in the way the questions are chosen and phrased and the manner in which they are asked. We can all give examples of questions that have been asked in a challenging or confrontational way. For example: 'Why have you left the gate open?' This elicits a defensive attitude in the response. Rather than doing this, choose questions carefully and learn to structure them so that they become valuable tools in the progression of your pupils, encouraging them to begin to think for themselves and take more responsibility for their own development.

SUMMARY

CHAPTER 2

■ COMMUNICATION IS PROBABLY THE KEY TO COACHING.

■ COACHING CAN ONLY BE ACHIEVED THROUGH GOOD COMMUNICATION SKILLS.

■ COMMUNICATE THROUGH VOICE, THROUGH BODY LANGUAGE, AND THROUGH 'LISTENING'.

■ QUESTIONS ESTABLISH COMMUNICATION AND ENSURE INVOLVEMENT.

■ CHOOSE QUESTIONS CAREFULLY AND USE THEM AS A VALUABLE TOOL OF COMMUNICATION.

TOP TIPS TOP TIPS TOP TIPS TOP TIPS

■ Ask questions throughout any training session – at the start and at intervals throughout the session – to sum up and ensure understanding. You will be amazed at how ongoing questions can lead and develop the coaching session as much as, or more than, any other 'tool' of coaching.

HOW PEOPLE LEARN

LEARNING MAY BE DEFINED AS ANY OF THE FOLLOWING: — TO GAIN KNOWLEDGE, SKILL OR ABILITY. — TO BE INFORMED (AND ABSORB THE INFORMATION). — A CHANGE OF BEHAVIOUR BROUGHT ABOUT BY EXPERIENCE.

Good and bad experiences

The last point in the list above is probably the most relevant to the riding experience. We hope that all the riders we work with will have a 'good experience'; however, at some stage in their career most riders will encounter something that leaves them with a 'bad experience'. Whether it is a fall from a horse, losing control of a horse, being run away with, or even something as apparently trivial as having a foot trodden on, that 'bad' experience may colour their opinion of riding in the future and even permanently. We have all come across the person who says: 'Oh, I went riding once – the horse bit me and ran away with me, and I've hated horses ever since.'

It is therefore essential that the way in which we teach riders and conduct lessons (especially for more novice riders) gives them a 'good experience' as consistently as possible. The 'bad experience', which may still happen, should be dealt with in a positive, constructive and supportive way so that the long-term effect of that experience is minimised and the outcome still has a positive element.

'Bad experiences' should be dealt with in a positive, supportive way.

Different outcomes

Let's look at examples of different learning outcomes based on a first canter lesson.

Preparations to ensure that the pupil has a good experience

• Careful choice of the horse/pony, to give the pupil an easy ride for this particular work.

• The instructor is fully aware of how to develop the first canter safely.

• The location for the exercise is a safe, enclosed area or an easy uphill slope out on a quiet hack.

• There is appropriate build-up work at the start of the lesson to ensure that the rider is riding well enough *today* to progress.

• The rider is confident and enthusiastic and keen to try the new exercise.

Outcome 1 (good experience)

• Rider experiences a first canter easily and is keen to further that experience.

Circumstances which might promote a very different outcome

• The horse or pony chosen is too spirited or 'sharp' for a less experienced rider.

• The pupil is one of a large group with an inexperienced instructor who is not sufficiently aware of the inadequacies of the pupil(s).

• There is not enough control of the group so horses/ponies are inclined to make their own decisions rather than be under the full control of their riders.

• The rider lacks confidence or is not showing enough riding ability or control to progress to trying canter *today*.

Outcome 2 (bad experience)

• The rider has a rather scary experience of a horse/pony running away in canter, which may result in a loss of balance, loss of one or more stirrups or at worst a fall.

• The rider is reluctant or scared to try the canter on a future occasion because the memory of the first attempt was not a happy one.

As instructors, it is essential that to the best of our ability we provide a good, happy, comfortable experience to our pupil(s) whenever possible. That is more likely to happen if lessons are well planned and we are always aware of the circumstances that maintain our riders' confidence and enthusiasm.

To help riders progress in their ability it is also important to challenge them and test them, but you can assess how far to challenge and test a person by QUESTIONING AND LISTENING and by assessing BODY LANGUAGE.

The learning process

Whether you are definitively 'coaching' or 'teaching' you must facilitate learning. Therefore, as a teacher/coach, it is your role to:

• Provide an environment which encourages your pupil(s) to learn.

• Enable your pupil(s) to take in information, to understand, process and practise.

• Have a variety of strategies to enable your pupil(s) to develop practical and theoretical skills.

It will be evident from these points that, if we are to do our jobs effectively, it is important to understand something about *how people learn*. There are some recognised models of this process. While these models emphasise different facets of the process, this does not mean that they are contradictory – indeed, a study of them will show that many of the ideas proposed work in parallel and reinforce each other. Let's have a look at them and see what information we can gain that will help the coaching process.

Skill development

• *Have you ever thought about how a skill is developed?*

Can you remember learning to walk or talk as a child? (I rather doubt it.) These two skills were developed progressively but through copying 'automatically'.

When a child tries to play tennis for the first time he picks up the racquet (perhaps correctly or very probably in a totally random way) then hits the ball and it travels 'somewhere'. At this stage the child is demonstrating:

1. Unconscious incompetence

- He has no technical knowledge of how to achieve his aim.

- He is totally unaware of how much there is to know about tennis.

A complete beginner on the leading rein.

• He has no awareness of how little he knows.

• He just wants to 'have a go' perhaps because he has seen someone else 'do it'.

He may have some degree of success (he may hit the ball) through basic hand–eye co-ordination and a desire to achieve.

This 'child' is our rider who has seen a friend riding and wants to 'have a go too'. The child (let's say beginner rider now) takes riding lessons and quickly moves from the state of *unconscious incompetence* to the next stage.

2. Conscious incompetence

After a few lessons our rider:

• Develops a clear awareness of how much there is to this 'riding sport'. (This awareness is more highly developed in an adult beginner than in a child, who still maintains a large degree of *unconscious incompetence*.)

• Becomes very aware of the need for co-ordination of 'aids'.

A novice rider who has had a few lessons.

• Develops understanding of the need to have effect and authority on the horse.

• Realises that to achieve the aim of a harmonious, effective partnership with the horse on the flat and over fences is considerably more difficult that it looks!

This is our rider who discovers what a steep hill he or she has set out to climb and that, at this stage, the support of the instructor is essential. The pupil's progress must be facilitated by setting realistic aims and small goals so that motivation is maintained and the rider is directed towards sustained development and sense of achievement.

Gradually, from this stage the rider moves towards stage 3.

3. Conscious competence

• Our rider begins to feel in control of various aspects of the work.

• Conscious competence may come in some areas of the work before it is achieved in other areas.

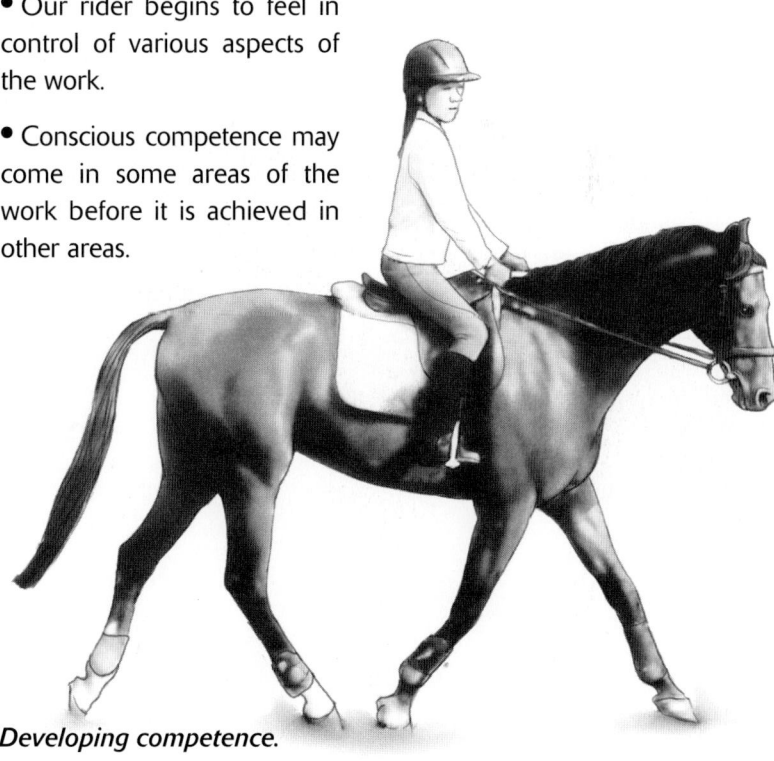

Developing competence.

• On the whole, as one aspect of the work moves into this state, then a new area of work can be introduced or developed.

• The rider's confidence is generally increased as conscious competence develops.

• Self-esteem and sense of achievement are increased, and this in turn contributes to more effort and commitment and more competence.

As the work becomes more 'automatic' the final stage is reached.

4. Unconscious competence

This is the 'doing-it-automatically-without-having-to-think-how' stage. Most of us drive cars in this state!

A highly competent rider at a major competition.

● An experienced rider should be in this stage. His or her interaction with the horse is 'second nature' and does not require a conscious thought process of preparation. The communication with the horse is therefore much quicker with a more harmonious, visible outcome.

● This state can be variable: if the rider does not practise and maintain the skill he or she may revert to the previous stage of competence (conscious).

It will be evident from this progression that PRACTICE is essential at each stage of learning and the rate of learning (developing competence) will be dictated to some degree by the frequency of the practice. In other words, we can say that RIDING IS LEARNED BY RIDING. While it is beneficial for a rider to have sound theoretical knowledge of 'what I am trying to do' on the horse, ultimately a rider's skill will only develop and improve by the actual 'doing'. Confucius is quoted (in 450 BC) as making the following statement:

What I hear I forget.

What I see I remember.

What I do I understand.

Kolb's model

In the 1970s, the educationalist David Kolb developed the concept of the experiential learning cycle. Like the skill development model, Kolb's model also suggests four stages of learning and it shows how learning develops through practical experience. Let's look at its progression, with an emphasis on the role of the coach.

1. Experiencing

• Every time someone rides they practise their skill or technique. They will use current input from the instructor/coach or may utilise past learning experience. Depending on the level of the rider, a session may be instructor/coach-led or rider-led (see Assessing Pupils, later this chapter, and Chapter 7).

• In every riding session you should be encouraging your pupil(s) to be considering their own experience. From this experience they can build their knowledge and awareness of their own progress.

• Questions within the session and at the end of the session will confirm riders' understanding of the work.

2. Reviewing

• You should 'review' each lesson and encourage your riders to do the same.

• Consider what was successful; which exercises improved horse and rider?

• What work was not so successful and why?

• Consider outside influences and how they could have been managed to produce a different outcome.

• Question the riders to find out their opinions and feelings of what you observed.

3. Concluding

• Resulting from the review of a lesson, conclusions should be drawn.

• Conclusions may affect your future strategy for the next session with that pupil.

• Conclusions must be drawn from your pupils' input as well as your own.

4. Planning

(See also Chapter 6.)

• Your role here as the coach is to plan and develop a training session as a result of previous experience.

• Your pupils' input is also valuable in the planning of future training.

Neuro-Linguistic Programming

In addition to acknowledging the skill development progression described earlier in this chapter, Neuro-Linguistic Programming (NLP) studies the ways in which people 'make sense' of their experiences in their own, individual, terms and recognises that a major means of processing experience is through our senses:

Auditory (hearing)/Visual (seeing)/Kinaesthetic (feeling)/Gustatory (tasting)/Olfactory (smelling). Although the last two have limited application to the learning of riding, we all have preferences for how we like to process information.

If your primary processing style is:

Auditory
you prefer verbal instruction, talking things through with your teacher.

Visual
you prefer to be shown what to do; you like to see what is meant.

Kinaesthetic
you like to 'try it'; you have to get a 'feel' for it; you like *participating* in an activity.

With reference to these descriptions:

• *Can you identify your own preferred processing style?*

• *Consider some of the pupils you know and teach regularly. Can you identify more or less readily with their processing styles?*

• *Think about some of the things you do regularly in lessons you teach. What exercises focus primarily on giving a pupil visual experiences? Kinaesthetic experiences? Auditory experiences?*

Honey and Mumford's model

The educationalists Honey and Mumford consider that people fall into categories in the way they *prefer* to learn, and they identify four main categories of learners. These are based, in part, on the wider attitudes of the individual, and understanding how these attitudes influence a pupil's learning can be crucial to effective coaching. If we consider ourselves as learners as well as teachers, then we will probably recognise ourselves in one or more of these categories (I have found, personally, that there is almost always some overlap).

• When you see a new activity about which you know very little, but perhaps you have always fostered a hidden desire to try, do you:

1. Want to get in there and 'have a go' as soon as you have observed the practice, irrespective of any theoretical understanding?

2. Want to 'have a go' and find out for yourself if 'it works'?

3. Want to watch the procedure and see someone else 'try it first'?

4. Want to know all about 'how to do it'; the underpinning detail and the theory behind the activity before even considering 'doing it'?

If you relate most to:

No. **1.** – you are an 'ACTIVIST'

No. **2.** – you are a 'PRAGMATIST'

No. **3.** – you are a 'REFLECTOR'

No. **4.** – you are a 'THEORIST'

(These points have certain links to the processing styles discussed in the section on Neuro-Linguistic Programming. For instance, comparisons can often be drawn between the kinaesthetic person and the activist, or the visual person and the pragmatist.)

Identifying and understanding your pupil(s)' preferred learning style(s) will help you considerably in keeping them satisfied when you are teaching them. In a group lesson, where pupils have different learning styles, it may not be possible to accommodate them all, completely, all of the time, but at least if you have an awareness of the differences in your pupils, you can begin to consider how you might best deliver your teaching.

Two scenarios

In the light of this, let's consider two practical coaching scenarios.

Scenario 1: Group jumping lesson

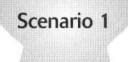

• Your class consists of six riders, all of whom have had some jumping experience, and today you are introducing a grid with three elements, which is new to most of them.

• Three riders are very keen and vie with each other to be first to ride the developing exercise.

Some riders are happier than others to be 'the first to go'.

• Two riders are happy to go towards the end of the group.

• One rider is always keen to go last and prefers to watch the others jump the new exercise two or three times before wanting to 'have a go'.

The preferred learning style of your riders is probably as follows:

• Your three keen, 'go-first' riders are *activists*.

• Your next two riders are predominantly *pragmatists*.

• Your rider who is happy to watch and then go eventually is probably a *theorist* or a *reflector*.

If you try to insist that the theorist/reflector goes first then you may disturb that rider enough that the outcome is not comfortable for them and they lose confidence. Similarly, if you spend too long expounding the theory of 'how to jump and why it will be this way or that', your activists will be bored and frustrated. By the time you let them jump not only will they have not taken in any of your theory, but also they will be tense and not in a focused state to jump well.

Scenario 2: Theory session

If you have a class full of 'activists' and you sit them in a lecture room and give hours of theoretical information about riding, are they going to be motivated and enthusiastic at the end of the session?

However, if you have one or two riders who love to study the 'why' and 'how', then sometimes they may be very happy to learn some of the theory of equitation (especially if it is cold and wet outside!). These learners will feel stimulated and satisfied even if they have not actually been 'doing'.

This consideration of learning styles should clarify for you why some of your riders love to talk for hours about 'how' and 'why'. Other riders in the meantime will give you a glazed expression, switching off as soon as you start to explain theory. Without going to extremes (i.e. *all* practice or *all* theory) you must learn to recognise the different learning styles of your pupils and try to adapt your teaching accordingly.

If you are giving a private lesson or are dealing with only one or two pupils at a time, it is much easier to identify their individual needs and direct your teaching more towards their preferred learning style – although, as I've said, you do need to give some consideration to their needs, as well as their preferences.

Developing teaching/coaching styles

It is a recognised fact that, as personalities, we tend to gravitate towards the person who delivers training in the way that we prefer to receive it. An extension of this concept is that, as an instructor/coach you will tend to develop your own style and this is likely to reflect the way that *you* like to be taught. Nevertheless, as we have seen throughout this chapter, it is beneficial to your pupils (and to your own development as a coach) that you are able to adapt through a range of styles to best accommodate the needs of your pupils. In a nutshell, for pupils to learn they must be receptive to your teaching. They must want to learn and they must participate in the learning experience.

Assessing pupils

How you facilitate learning for any individual will depend on many factors. We have already discussed the need to understand some of the overall learning *processes,* but there are also some fundamental questions which need to be answered in respect of each pupil.

• How much does the pupil already know?

• How much new information do they need?

• How will your pupil react or cope if they 'get it wrong'?

• How many experiences can you give them to practise what you are teaching? The best learning experience is one of great depth, breadth and variety, but:

• How much can they 'learn' in one session?

• Do you need to consider the environment in which the learning is taking place? (Health and safety.)

Almost certainly, your teaching style will need to be adapted according to the *ability* of your pupil(s).

• A novice or inexperienced rider needs much new information and support. The coach's input will therefore be extensive because the skills need to be 'taught' in detail. This work is *coach led.*

• A rider who is developing some skill and has a level of competence and confidence in some areas will need less specific input and will often be able to direct his or her own work and progress. While there will still be some 'teaching' there will also be some independent 'finding out'. Here there is a balance between the work being *coach led* and *rider led.*

• An assured, experienced rider who is able to regulate his or her own programme will need your opinions on how the work is appearing and may require some fine-tuning to improve the performance. There will be less 'technical teaching' and more discussion of what the coach is seeing against what the rider is feeling and then how things could be adapted to reach mutual agreement. Here the work is *rider led.*

(These concepts will be explored more fully in Chapter 7.)

It is important that you, as the coach, are able to adapt from a style of total support for the novice or nervous, inexperienced rider, to a style of advice and guidance for the established, self-sufficient rider.

Empowering pupils

Your greatest achievement as a coach is to *empower* your client to achieve competence in your absence. Ultimately, the rider who is completely in control of his or her development and performance without your support is the rider who is able to compete with confidence and win as a result of that confidence.

The competitive rider who believes that he or she is able to win is a strong competitor to beat. The variable link in our sport is the horse (for a number of reasons, he may not have his 'winning hat' on), but the more confident the rider, the more he or she will instil confidence in the horse and the greater the likelihood that this will lead the partnership to success.

 ## Points to ponder

Here are some questions to help you focus on points raised in this chapter:

- *What is your preferred style of teaching?*

- *How often do you adapt your teaching style for different pupils?*

- *How much do you question your riders within a session, to confirm their understanding and therefore plan further progress?*

- *How do you ensure that your rider(s) are working as hard at their development as you are?*

- *How much do you empower your riders to perform without you being there to support them?*

SUMMARY

CHAPTER 3

■ HOW DO YOU 'LEARN'? CONSIDER HOW YOUR PUPILS LEARN.

■ LEARNING MAY BE ACHIEVED THROUGH 'WATCHING', 'FEELING', 'HEARING', AND 'DOING'.

■ TEACHING IS ACHIEVED THROUGH 'TELLING', 'SHARING', AND 'ALLOWING'.

TOP TIPS TOP TIPS TOP TIPS TOP TIPS

■ If one teaching style is not achieving the results you had hoped for, then be able to adapt your style to approach the session from a different angle, which can revitalise and move the lesson on again.

CHAPTER 4

AWARENESS AND JUDGEMENT

I BELIEVE THAT FOR A SPORTS COACH, AND PARTICULARLY IN EQUESTRIAN SPORT WHERE THE HORSE IS ALSO A MAJOR PLAYER, THESE TWO WORDS ARE AS CRUCIAL AND VALUABLE AS ANY IN OUR VOCABULARY.

> • *What does awareness mean and how does it apply in our day-to-day teaching?*
>
> • *What is judgement and when do we need to use it?*

Awareness means a state of 'consciousness', being 'informed' and being 'wary'.

Judgement means (among many other things!) 'reasoning', 'comparing ideas to form opinions'.

In the highly litigious world in which we now live, it is absolutely imperative that you as a riding instructor/coach can stand by every decision and choice you make with regard to your pupils' welfare while riding. Throughout my career I have always considered the welfare of my pupils to be of paramount importance. I truly believe that, should I ever be called to justify a choice I made for a rider (because it had resulted in 'an accident'), I would be able to stand up and declare that I had made the choice I did based on *awareness* and with *judgement* for the circumstances at the time.

Developing awareness as a coach

Riding *is* a risk sport, in spite of everything. In riding an animal weighing around half a ton, who has a mind of his own, often at speed and sometimes over obstacles, there is the potential for incidents and accidents. Third party and environmental influences can add to the risk.

I believe we have an obligation to ensure that riders and those responsible for them know, at the outset, that riding is a sport that can produce the unexpected, and while every care will be taken to minimise the risk of any incidents, these cannot be ruled out completely.

Awareness develops with experience and there is no short cut to our own 'learning from experience'. However, it is important to ensure that, to best of your ability, your pupils' welfare is safeguarded.

Risk assessment before lessons

I mentioned earlier about the need to minimise risk when teaching. The ability to make a 'risk assessment' competently before every lesson you teach should become ingrained. If you always teach in the same environment then this is relatively easy. You make a risk assessment of the area in which you will be teaching and within reason that can follow through for days, weeks or even months as long as nothing changes. (That said, minor variables, such as the effect of weather conditions, do have to be considered constantly.) If you teach in a different venue perhaps every day (because you are a travelling freelance instructor) then you must be able to risk-assess each situation on its own merits.

Things that you might consider in a risk assessment of an arena in which you are going to take an individual flatwork lesson could include the following:

• Access to arena (where would your rider approach from – stables, car park, through a gate/sliding door?)

- Outside distraction in proximity to arena. (Busy road alongside, field with horses turned out, who might gallop about.)

- Type of arena surface.

- Lights (or lack of them); light conditions generally.

- Jump materials stacked in the corners?

- Access into the school from, for example, the gallery or outside.

- Spectators (e.g. in the school/outside the school but audible/outside the school behind glass).

These are just a few main factors that might be included in a risk assessment and your *awareness* of how any of these factors *might* affect your lesson could be relevant if an incident arose in which a rider was injured.

Let us consider two scenarios taking into account the seven points I have referred to above.

A safe environment.

Scenario 1

• You allow your pupil and his horse to come into the school from a busy car park and leave the door open as they start working in.

• There is a field alongside the school and three horses have just been turned out and are galloping around having a wild time.

• The school surface is bark chippings and the watering system was left on too long and the bark is very wet and slippery.

• It is early evening in October and only three of the six lights are working in the school so there are large patches of shadow, especially near two corners.

• There are some jump materials left untidily in one of the dark corners.

• You have started to work your rider without stirrups and the horse is rather full of himself.

• A spectator from the open gallery walks without warning into the school through a small door in a dark corner just as the rider approaches.

• The horse spooks at the spectator, slips on the bark and frightens himself by stumbling against the loose poles in the corner. He then shies away, drops his shoulder and the rider falls off.

If the rider sustained an injury from this incident, YOUR total lack of awareness for the potential risks in the whole situation would render you very vulnerable to an accusation of lack of care (negligence).

Scenario 2

• You ensure that the rider comes into the school from the busy car park probably leading the horse, with stirrups run up and reins over the horse's head. He mounts in the school, having first closed the door.

• You either request that the horses are not in the field while the lesson is going on, or advise the pupil to be *'aware'* of the possible distraction and also ensure that the ridden horse is aware of the loose horses.

• You do not work the rider without stirrups: (a) because of the loose horses; (b) because of the slippery surface.

• You ensure that the rider is *aware* of the wet surface so that he can adapt his riding accordingly.

• You restack the jump materials so that they are tidy and safe.

• If you consider the surface to be too slippery to work in canter you keep the work in walk and trot.

Ideally, if you have prior notice of the facts and the time and opportunity to influence them:

• You ensure that there is a notice in the gallery to advise spectators that NO ONE must enter the school from the gallery while a lesson is in progress. (If you can't arrange a notice, politely request that any spectators do not do this.)

• You make sure that the lights are repaired before you teach. If this is not achievable, you work the horse in the lightest area of the school. Or (if you consider it safe) you work the horse at walk in the dark area of the school and at trot in the light end.

In this second scenario it is hoped that the circumstances would not lead to the horse spooking and the fall would be avoided. The two scenarios are very different only because of the *awareness* of the instructor/coach and the *judgement* used within the lesson.

Ongoing awareness and judgement

It is your job to ensure that you use *judgement* and are constantly *aware* of how a session is developing and progressing. In all your teaching situations, try to be *aware* of:

• Facilities (access/condition/space availability/changing circumstances).

• Surroundings (weather/outside influences).

Use *judgement* for:

• Choice of work – difficulty and intensity.

• Development of exercises depending on how situations evolve.

• If in doubt, *don't*!

Remember, however, that a permanently cautious attitude will ultimately make your pupils less safe because they lack practical application. 'Riding is learnt by riding'. Your pupils must 'do' and 'experience' to learn.

Consider the following statement and then again we will look at two scenarios to illustrate the statement:

'It is unsafe to teach a rider on the lunge without reins and stirrups.'

Scenario 1

Scenario 1

• You are lungeing an unfamiliar horse with a rider you have never taught before; you are in a school in which you have never taught before.

• The rider has not worked without reins before, although he has worked without stirrups.

• The rider is unfamiliar with you and does not appear to be very confident; he is reluctant to try anything 'new'.

• In spite of this you take away his reins and stirrups and he 'survives' the experience but is not keen to ride with you in the future!

Scenario 2

• You are lungeing a school horse of your own, who you have worked with countless times before, and you are in your own school.

• Your pupil is a rider you have taught for many years. You started his training on a pony on the lunge and he has ridden this horse many times both loose and on the lunge.

• This rider has lost count of how many times he has ridden without reins or stirrups.

• Today you suggest that he might try working without both reins and stirrups and he is very keen.

• The outcome is positive and motivating for the rider, who has achieved a new level of competence and confidence.

Referring to the original statement, in scenario 1 the statement might be appropriate; but in scenario 2 it would not be applicable. The whole situation is affected by *awareness* and *judgement*.

Capable pupil working on the lunge without stirrups.

Developing awareness in the rider

Children who grow up in an environment where there are animals of any kind will have a far greater innate *'awareness'* of animal behaviour and unpredictability than those who come from an animal-free background.

It is your responsibility as an instructor to enhance an existing awareness and where necessary instil and develop awareness in those for whom that characteristic is not natural.

Through your *awareness* and *judgement* you will display a progression in the work that is appropriate at any stage of your pupils' riding experience.

It is essential that throughout the teaching sessions:

• You encourage your riders to *question* what they are doing – when and why.

• You encourage your riders to consider the implications of the choices they make, or that you make on their behalf.

• You encourage your riders to compare themselves with other riders of similar experience to make decisions about their own standard and capability.

• Relating to these factors there will also be some influence from the innate self-confidence or bravery of the individual rider and there will be some relevance to the horse they are riding.

• Ultimately you want your riders, whatever their level, to be confident in their awareness of what they are doing and feel in control of the situation.

• Your riders gradually develop an enhanced *awareness* of their own capability and become more confident in their own *judgement* of their ability.

Developing *awareness* and *judgement* in your pupils empowers them to be independent of you, the coach. This is your ultimate achievement as a coach – they are then able to perform to their maximum competence without any reliance on you.

Understanding

- *What is understanding?*
- *Is learning achieved if there is not understanding?*

Understanding is achieving a grasp of the meaning of an explanation. It is an awareness of how to do something. A good coach ensures that his or her pupil understands because, without understanding, the pupil is not enlightened with knowledge of how, why or when. The pupil is therefore not empowered through understanding to be in control and safe.

Without understanding, the pupil is copying or mimicking a procedure carried out by another person – but, without understanding, this could prove to be hazardous or even harmful. A trained rider jumping a fence will ensure control and judgement of things like speed, direction of approach and awareness of terrain and thus negotiate the obstacle safely. A brave, observant non-rider could climb onto a horse and aim at a fence with total lack of understanding of what is really involved, with the result that the rider and/or the horse are seriously injured.

Levels of understanding

Let's consider a person who wishes to ride (may have seen a friend or relative ride) and decides to take a riding lesson. We'll look at this in the terms used to describe skill development in the previous chapter.

Unconscious incompetence

Our would-be rider is totally unaware of:

✦ How difficult riding is as a sport.
✦ How little they know.
✦ How much there is to know.
✦ How much co-ordination is required.
✦ How much physical effort is involved.
✦ How much concentration is required.
✦ How much mental application is needed.
✦ How scary it can be.
✦ How fulfilling and fun it is.

Our newcomer is blissfully unaware and is *unconsciously incompetent*. Moving on, he joins a regular class.

Conscious incompetence

✦   The beginner rider suddenly discovers how much there is to learn about this new sport he has embraced.
✦   He becomes aware of how little he knows.
✦   He begins to study the sport and the more he learns the more he realises there is to learn.

He becomes *consciously* aware of how *incompetent* he is.

If the rider gets past the consciously incompetent stage, he then begins to move into the next stage.

Conscious competence

✦   Here, the rider is developing some skill. However, note that skills may evolve at different rates so a rider may be quite competent in some areas, but less so in others.
✦   As he becomes more competent each skill becomes more fluent and 'automatic'.

✦ Some skills still require much concentration to achieve; these are not yet 'automatic'.

But our rider is improving all the time…moving into the realms of:

Unconscious competence

✦ The skill is now so familiar that it is 'automatic'. The rider does not need to think and consider how he will act/react (e.g. what aids to use for a specific movement).

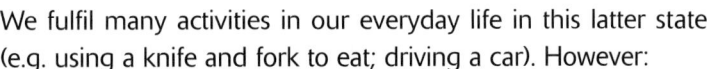

We fulfil many activities in our everyday life in this latter state (e.g. using a knife and fork to eat; driving a car). However:

● *Have you tried to eat with chopsticks?*

● *Can you remember learning to do something completely new?*

These levels of competence relate to understanding; they are also relevant to 'how we teach' (see previous chapter).

The beginner at the first stage will need much help and guidance in order to:

1. Learn.
2. Understand.
3. Develop skill and confidence.

Such a rider will need structured teaching which involves a large input of '*telling*'. He or she will have to have lessons which are *coach led* (see Chapter 7).

The rider who is a *conscious incompetent* will still need lessons which are predominantly *coach led*. The lessons will be planned and structured by the coach, with much input from the coach. However, here should be an evolving flow of information from the rider, as the coach invites the pupil to begin to 'input' more into the lesson. There is some *sharing* between coach and pupil and the rider's feedback should help to guide the way in which the coach develops the lesson.

The rider who is a *conscious competent* will have developed some independent skills and often a desire to 'experiment' with different techniques and training principles. This rider should be having considerable input into the lesson content through liaison with the coach. There is much *sharing* in the way the lesson is planned and developed.

The *unconscious competent* rider is well established and riding with independence and confidence. Such riders will often be competing. They need to have training sessions which are largely *rider led*. The coach is there to advise, guide and hone the existing ability. The session should have a great deal of rider input from the start. The rider may discuss methods and training principles in depth. The coach's role may take on other aspects, which we will consider later in this chapter under sport psychology.

The experienced coach will be able to adapt through these four permutations of teaching methods and be highly flexible in recognising the appropriate circumstances, adopting the style most helpful to the rider at that specific time.

Scenarios

Let us consider some hypothetical scenarios and match the appropriate teaching style.

1. Beginner rider (child), first riding lesson – *unconscious incompetent*.

Lesson will be *coach led*. The lesson will have plan, structure, much initial 'teaching' of new techniques, e.g. mounting and how to hold the reins. The work will be closely monitored and there will be minimal rider input in directing the lesson.

2. Child rider can rise to the trot and ride in walk and trot unaided *(developing conscious competence in those fields)* **but has yet to experience his first canter.**

This rider is developing skill in trot and is consciously aware of how much he can do in these areas: he can begin to enjoy developing competence in walk and trot. With regard to canter, if he has not seen other people doing it, he is still *unconsciously incompetent* (he can't yet do it, but is unaware of this). If he has seen other people doing it, then he will be *consciously incompetent* – aware that it is something he has not yet done, and is not sure how to do. This skill will still need to be 'taught' with full input from the coach. This lesson should have a mixture of 'tell' and 'share'.

3. Adult rider, rode years ago to quite a good level, has had a break from riding and is now starting lessons again after a gap of many years.

This rider probably was unconsciously competent but because of the time gap in practising the skills he will almost certainly have dropped from that state back to the conscious competent, or even to the conscious incompetent. He will need much guidance and revision to re-establish his level of skill, and often this is closely linked to the confidence level of the person. The coach will probably need to guide the session predominantly.

Physical ability and fitness

These topics should be intrinsic to the awareness and judgement of a riding coach. Consideration of physical ability and fitness should influence:

+ Allocation of riders to horses.
+ What can reasonably be expected of riders.
+ What can reasonably be expected of horses.
+ In some cases, whether a trainer/coach should ride a pupil's horse.

Ability and fitness of pupils

In coaching riders we are involved in equestrian sport. All sports require some degree of physical ability and fitness. The level of fitness of the 'athlete' will depend on the intensity and the level of the sport. Sometimes, in equestrian activities (certainly at the more novice levels), riders consider that it is the horse's responsibility to be 'fit' to carry the rider – and, of course, this is the case. The rider, however, has a huge responsibility also to be fit enough to participate fully in the riding experience and not just be a 'body' that the horse has to carry about for the duration of the lesson.

- *As the coach, how do you assess and consider the rider's physical ability?*

- *Is it necessary and relevant to consider the rider's conformation?*

- *Is it appropriate to discuss fitness with your riders?*

- *Is it relevant to consider which horse you might mount a particular rider on, in view of that rider's conformation and physical ability?*

As both an instructor/coach and also an active rider/competitor I have always been very committed to my own personal fitness. I have always tried to instil self-discipline and awareness into all my pupils, whatever their level and aspirations. Riding is a sport and to carry out any sport effectively some level of physical fitness is essential. Physical fitness also conveys mental fitness and this can enhance concentration, co-ordination and focus, all attributes which will improve the physical ability to ride.

- Considering the physical ability of each rider (on initial meeting or first lesson) will help to ensure that you use appropriate judgement in the choice, intensity and length of the work you choose for the rider.

● It is important that riders are encouraged to be aware of their own fitness with regard to the sport (riding) that they have chosen. Ongoing discussion and advice on the progressive development of fitness may be helpful. Often the rider may not even have given the subject consideration. Questions about alternative activities may reveal participation in exercise such as dog-walking, swimming, jogging, cycling, line dancing, yoga, Pilates (the list is endless). Emphasis needs to be put on the value of any such activities and their relevant importance to the rider.

● Similar discussion about diet may also prove helpful (especially with children). Healthy eating and, more importantly, adequate fluid intake will enhance the rider's physical ability. Water is the most valuable drink for any athlete; enhancement with electrolytes may be helpful too (riders may be unaware of just how much fluid they lose through their bodies while riding and regular replacement prevents a risk of dehydration). In my opinion no rider should be without some form of fluid available to them during and after a riding session (especially in hot weather).

● A rider who carries excess weight (especially a child or adolescent) needs extremely tactful and careful consideration. A thoughtless or badly timed comment can be enough to tip a young person towards eating disorders. This is extremely dangerous ground and the coach needs to be well informed and know the rider well before offering opinions that could have a lasting effect on a rider's behaviour. If in doubt where a child/adolescent is concerned, talk to a parent or guardian before broaching the subject with the individual.

● If you are running a training centre or riding school it is possible that the establishment will have a policy in place that dictates a weight limit for riders.

● Considering the rider's physique or conformation is sensible and can be done unobtrusively; it should nevertheless be part of internal policy in a good riding school or training establishment. Mounting a novice rider with short legs and broad thighs on a big-moving, wide, broad-backed, but lazy horse will not give the rider much chance. The rider with such a conformation would be better suited on a slight, narrow, lighter type of horse with less movement but more natural inclination to go forward.

• While having an ideal picture in your mind of the rider in a 'good balanced position' on the horse, conformation must be taken into account. If a rider has short arms, constant requests to 'shorten your reins' will produce a rider with stiff arms and limited flexibility in the elbow, or with a tendency to tip forward to maintain a shorter, more consistent rein contact. Because the rider has short arms, it may be best for them to have their reins a little longer while maintaining balance in the saddle and flexibility in the arm/hand position and therefore better rein contact. A rider with naturally longer arms can adopt a more 'ideal' elbow/forearm/wrist elasticity.

• While coaching, ensure that you constantly review the effect of the work you are doing on your pupil(s). It is easy to become so enthusiastic in your teaching and in your efforts to keep your rider(s) busy and satisfied, that you forget to consider how they are coping physically.

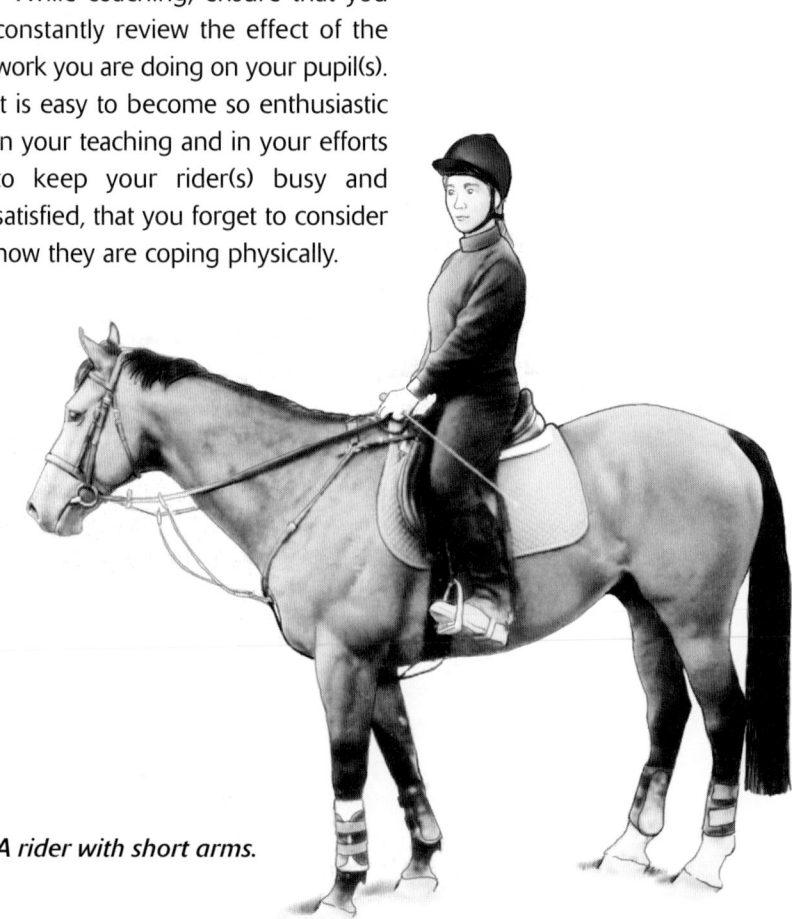

A rider with short arms.

• Remember that weather conditions will affect the work you may achieve with both horses and riders. On a very hot or humid day the fitness of both horses and riders will be challenged much earlier than on a cooler day.

• It is easy to forget how fit you personally may be (because you work with horses all day and every day, you muck out five a day, ride three and teach four hours a day!). Some of your pupils may ride only once a week, and in between lessons they may take NO other form of physical activity at all! They will not be very fit and too much work ultimately may be damaging both to them and to the horse who has to carry them when they lose balance and co-ordination through fatigue.

• Use *questions* to find out from your rider(s) how they feel at various stages through any training session. Learn to read your rider(s): they may say they are fine, but you know different.

A well-proportioned rider.

Your *awareness* and *judgement* will ensure that any session you are coaching is regulated according to the physical fitness of your riders.

Fitness of the coach

We have spent some time considering the physical ability of our riders/pupils.

• *What about your fitness?*

   How fit do you consider yourself to be?
   How fit do you need to be to be able to teach/coach?

• *Should you be able to ride any horse; should you be able to sort out problems from the ground, or should you ride the horse if there are difficulties?*

Regarding the first question, by virtue of the occupation I think it is fairly unlikely that most riding instructors/coaches will not be physically fit. However, someone who was previously an accomplished rider, and has coaching skills, but is now precluded from active riding for age/health reasons, may still be very valuable as a coach, despite their physical state.

The question about riding any horse gives rise to a point which (while perhaps going off on a tangent) is pertinent to how coaching is defined in practical terms. Equestrian sport coaches choose to teach riding *usually* because at some stage they have ridden or still do ride themselves. However, there is a line of thought that if you understand the process of coaching (e.g. how people take in information, learning styles, teaching skills, etc.) then *any* coach can coach *any* subject. I can agree with the broad philosophy of that idea, BUT a coach of any subject must also have technical knowledge of and *some* competence in that subject. Personally, I do not consider that, for example, a netball coach could come in with no knowledge of riding and 'teach' riding. That person may be able to 'coach' an already competent rider, helping that person develop motivation, planning, etc., but he or she would not be capable of helping an inexperienced rider attain greater skill competence, nor, in the current context, of 'getting on and showing them'.

Regarding trainers/coaches riding pupils' horses generally, I don't think is such a 'cut and dried' affair. Without doubt, it *can* be very helpful and motivating for a rider if the trainer/coach rides the horse and 'shows' the pupil how to achieve a higher level of work with him. But, in my opinion, there are many reasons both for and against riding horses for pupils within a training session, and the following are just some of them.

Advantages

• The horse may go considerably better for the trainer/coach, which can be motivating for the rider when he or she gets back on and feels the difference.

• The horse 'moves up a gear' by being ridden more effectively and the pupil may then be able to maintain that improvement because they have seen it and are challenged to achieve the same.

• The trainer/coach feels that they can achieve more in a shorter period by riding the horse and then putting the owner back on to feel the difference, than by trying to get the pupil to achieve the desired effect themselves. This also provides an opportunity to show and explain to the pupil what is being done.

• The trainer/coach is competent and fit and quite able to deal with any resistance that they may induce by challenging the horse to go differently.

Disadvantages

● The rider may, in fact, be very able and the issue is not whether the trainer/coach personally can influence the horse any better, but is trying to find a way to help the rider achieve success with a new exercise – in which case the coach is more valuable as an observer on the ground.

● The trainer/coach produces a way of going from the horse that the pupil is not able to maintain and the horse then feels he can 'do his own thing' and the pupil can't do much about it.

● The trainer/coach stirs up some resistance from the horse, perhaps because he is asked to go in a way that he has never had to before and, since he has not been challenged in this way, he resists. The owner then experiences the horse's disturbance even though, in the long term, the intervention should help the horse's overall development.

● The trainer/coach is no longer fit enough as a rider to tackle issues which are the domain of the athletic younger rider. (As we get older we are unwise to put ourselves in a situation where a young, opinionated horse might challenge our 'stickability'. Consideration should be given to how easily we break but are not so easy to mend!). Discretion becomes the better part of valour!

Another factor to consider when debating whether or not you need to ride a client's horse is that the more experienced you become as a coach, the easier it is to assess how best to help the rider from the ground.

Psychology of rider and horse

Sport psychology is now a huge and valuable subject in its own right and the psychology of the horse is an area that attracts an enormous amount of interest. The pure study of the psychology of both horse and rider is outside the remit of this book, but elsewhere readers can find a wealth of publications dedicated specifically to these topics.

However, the subject, with regard to both rider and horse, cannot go unmentioned, because it relates both to the fundamental aim of this book, to improve coaching skills, and also to the specific subject matter of this chapter. We have just seen that awareness of and judgements about the physical condition of pupils and horses are important aspects of coaching, and the same is true of their mental processes.

Psychology of the rider

Put simply, psychology is the study of the mind and behaviour – it relates to a person's characteristics and attitudes. These can be changed drastically by a horse! They can also be affected by the coach.

If we think about 'sport psychology' we are considering subjects such as:

+ Motivation.

+ Dealing with success and failure.

+ Goal-setting and achieving.

+ Mental preparation and visualisation.

+ Working as a team.

+ Developing the 'competitive edge'.

Further reference to these subjects will be made in Chapters 5, 6 and 10.

Psychology of the horse

I believe that as horse lovers (aren't we all?) we ignore horse psychology at our peril. Psychology of the horse is understanding what makes him 'tick'.

The horse would love to spend most of his time eating.

Remember:

+ The horse is a herd animal.
+ He is usually 'a follower' not so often a leader.
+ He is non-aggressive by nature.
+ He is an animal of 'flight'.
+ He is a herbivore and a 'browser'. (He would love to spend most of his life eating.)

As coaches of equestrian sport we have an ongoing and a huge responsibility to remember the origins and instincts of the wonderful animal who is our partner in our sporting activity. If we continually maintain awareness of his attitudes and characteristics then we will go a long way in developing the ultimate successful partnership with him in training the rider.

SUMMARY

CHAPTER 4

■ AWARENESS AND JUDGEMENT DEVELOP WITH EXPERIENCE, BUT LEARN TO 'FEEL' AND BE INSTINCTIVE IN YOUR COACHING; 'IF IN DOUBT, DON'T DO IT'.

■ UNDERSTANDING ENSURES INDEPENDENCE AND CONFIDENCE.

■ COMPETENCE DEVELOPS THROUGH STAGES AND CAN FLUCTUATE ACCORDING TO PRACTICE OF A SKILL.

■ PHYSICAL ABILITY AND FITNESS HAVE AN EMPHASIS: RIDING IS A 'SPORT'.

■ RIDER AND HORSE PSYCHOLOGY ARE RELEVANT TO DEVELOPING A PARTNERSHIP BETWEEN HORSE AND RIDER, AND THE COACH MAY BE THE KEY FACILITATOR.

TOP TIPS TOP TIPS TOP TIPS TOP TIPS

■ Show interest in your pupils. They will work with you far more easily if you find out what they feel and are keen to aim for, rather than if you put your own perspective on the lesson.

■ Awareness and judgement will help to ensure that appropriate choices are made with regard to exercises or work chosen.

■ Consider riders' physical ability and fitness.

■ Match conformation of rider to appropriate ease of ride of a horse where possible.

■ Consider riders' characteristics and attitudes to their riding.

■ Remember that the horse is a horse! Remember where he 'comes from'.

TAKING RESPONSIBILITY

IN COMMITTING YOURSELF TO A PROFESSION AS AN 'INSTRUCTOR' OR 'COACH', YOU PERSONALLY TAKE ON A HUGE RESPONSIBILITY, PARTICULARLY IF YOU ARE GOING TO BE TEACHING YOUNG PEOPLE AND CHILDREN. YOU WILL OFTEN BE SEEN IN A POSITION OF AUTHORITY AND THOSE PEOPLE WHOM YOU 'TEACH' WILL TAKE IN YOUR OPINIONS AND KNOWLEDGE. IN THIS RESPECT ALONE, YOU HAVE A *RESPONSIBILITY* TO ENSURE THAT, TO THE BEST OF YOUR ABILITY, THE INFORMATION YOU IMPART TO OTHERS IS CORRECT, UP TO DATE AND APPROPRIATE TO THE NEEDS OF YOUR PUPIL(S) AT ANY TIME. LET US EXPLORE THE CONCEPT OF *'TAKING RESPONSIBILITY'* A LITTLE FURTHER.

The coach's responsibility

- *How do you decide what to cover in any one lesson?*

- *How do you ensure that your riders are satisfied with their lesson?*

- *Is it your fault if your riders do not achieve the aims of the lesson?*

These questions can be considered and perhaps answered in this chapter.

In any lesson, learning can only be achieved (in a sustained way and in the long term) if there is a joint commitment from the pupil(s) and the coach. With this in mind it is essential to ask and answer the following questions at the beginning of any lesson:

- What are the rider's expectations of the lesson? (What do they want to work on or achieve within the session?)

- What is their past experience?

- How long is the lesson?

- What are the peripheral influences that might affect the lesson's outcome? (For example: rider tired after a day at school/work; rider had a row with parent/boyfriend/girlfriend before arriving to ride; windy day, horse turned out in adjacent field causing possible distraction, etc.)

The lesson that follows could have two very different outcomes depending on the knowledge obtained prior to its start.

Scenario 1

Scenario 1: Private lesson (one to one) with a teenage rider on her own horse; the pair have a one-day event at the weekend and the rider wants to 'brush up' for the competition.

Rider's perception (before the lesson, which mother has booked):

- 'Oh great, I've got a lesson on Thursday. I'll be able to jump as I haven't got any fences at home to practise over and I haven't jumped Fred since the last competition!'

- 'I must remember to tell Ann (coach) that I must practise my medium trot 'cos I got a 4 for that last time I competed!'

- 'Oh hell, I've got to hand in my maths homework first thing tomorrow, and I'm meeting Joe (boyfriend) tonight. Hope I can get Mum to put Fred away for me after my lesson!'

- 'Wonder what test I'm riding on Saturday. Hope Mum has remembered to look!'

Coach's perception (before the lesson, her last of a busy day):

- 'I've got Jan this evening. Hope she has worked the horse a bit since I last saw her. He was so sharp and full of himself because he hadn't had enough work; I don't know why her mother wastes her money! I had to spend the whole session getting him relaxed and loose enough to work.'

- 'I hope she doesn't want to jump. I want to leave work on time as I'm going out tonight and I don't want to have to put up a whole lot of jumps.'

- 'I expect she's got a competition coming up. I hope she knows the test this time.'

The lesson develops something like this:

- *Jan* arrives and starts working in. There is minimal communication between *Jan* (rider) and *Ann* (coach) and certainly there is no discussion about where the lesson should be going and what the expectations of the rider (or coach) are.

- *Ann* assesses the horse and rider and *decides* that the horse is not going as *she would want him* to.

- *Ann* then directs the lesson based entirely on what *she has assessed and decided*. She works the rider on the flat and makes no indication that the session will involve any jumping.

- *Jan* carries out the instruction given by Ann but *becomes increasingly frustrated*, because in *her* mind the lesson is not going *as she would have chosen it to go.*

The outcome of the lesson is wholly unsatisfactory (particularly for the rider) because it in no way fulfilled *the rider's expectations* (which were never discussed).

Scenario 2

Scenario 2: Same rider as above. Same thoughts of both rider and coach prior to the lesson.

If there is a JOINT RESPONSIBILITY for the outcome of the lesson, the lesson could go something like this:

At the beginning of the lesson, a series of information-gathering questions by the coach can clarify the aims and intentions of both pupil and coach:

- 'How are you, Jan? What have you been up to since we last met?'

- 'How is Fred going? What sort of work have you been doing with him?'

- 'How was your last competition? Where did you get your best marks in your test? (Oh, so you need to work a bit on the medium trot?)'

- 'Is there anything else you particularly want to work on today?'

- 'You want to jump, do you? Unfortunately I haven't got a course up but we could work on the flat to start with and see if we can improve the trot for your test, and then work on a grid towards the end. If we use some poles this will help his medium trot as well. Are you happy with that?'

- 'I need to be prompt finishing tonight so we need to get started. (Oh, that's fine; you are on a tight time schedule too. Good old Mum – no doubt she'll put Fred to bed for you!).'

This second scenario would have the following benefits:

- It would ensure that *prior* to the lesson rider and coach had discussed their joint aspirations about its purpose and content.

• *Jan* would not spend the next forty minutes riding around feeling frustrated that the time was slipping by and there was no sign that they might be jumping in the lesson.

• *Ann* would know how much the horse had been worked since they last met; and she would know the outcome of the last competition and what the rider wanted to work on this time.

• *Ann* would also feel that she had allowed for the lesson to finish punctually and could then concentrate on giving a helpful training session, within the agreed parameters of time and work to be covered.

• Satisfaction would be much more assured from both rider and pupil because of:

    ✦ A shared responsibility for the lesson.

    ✦ An agreed plan of what to cover during that session.

    ✦ The rider focusing on the plan because she was not worrying about 'what might happen in the lesson'.

The rider's responsibility

• *How often have you taught a lesson where, by the end, you feel drained and exhausted because your pupils have taken so much from you?*

• *How often have you worked harder and harder to achieve an outcome from a lesson?*

• *How often have you ended up in a situation where the harder you work the less your pupils do and the harder still you work?*

In all these cases, your pupils are putting all the responsibility on you for the satisfactory outcome of the lesson.

These days we live in a society where it is never 'my fault' if something goes wrong – it is always someone else's fault:

• *'Just as I entered the arena the wind got up and my horse gets spooky when it's windy.'*

• *'He worked in perfectly and then the judge was running late so he'd gone past his best and the test was awful!'*

• *'I didn't have enough time to work in because my dad got lost on the way so we were late!'*

The list of people, or situations, which cause the poor performance, or lack of satisfactory outcome, is endless!

Unless the rider learns to take responsibility then they will continue to 'fail' because they are not 'in control' of their own outcome.

As a coach it is up to you to hand a degree of responsibility over to your pupil(s) and then allow them to be in control of their own outcomes. This ultimately empowers them to be able to produce their best performance without you (their coach) being there.

Top athletes have this innate self-control; it may be developed and enhanced with careful assistance from their coach. With their own sense of responsibility for all they do, they are then very self-disciplined and this empowers them with a self-belief and confidence, which will give them the competitive edge needed to win. They are not directly dependent on anyone or anything for their success; they are in control of the whole situation so the outcome is their own. (The biggest variable in equestrian sport is the horse! The chances are, however, that because of the rider's horsemastership skills, confidence and authority, the horse will also be in a maximum state of performance and control. We will look further at the relationship between horse, rider and coach in the next section.)

How can we develop the rider's sense of effort to take responsibility and develop his or her own skills with the coach's assistance, but while not being *dependent* on the coach?

Whether you know the rider(s) or not (i.e. whether you have prior knowledge of ability, confidence, attitude and aptitude):

✦ At the start of every lesson you should ask questions.

✦ Throughout your session you should ask questions.

✦ When you are unsure of what the rider(s) might be thinking or feeling (it may be nothing!), you should ask questions.

Perceptive coaching empowers riders to produce their best performances without the coach being there.

As we saw in Chapter 2, questions can be your most valuable tool; they certainly become your greatest asset in communicating with your pupil(s).

• By asking questions and listening to the answer(s) you can formulate your lesson structure or plan and decide how best to take the lesson forward.

• Your rider(s) will feel involved in your decisions about the way forward.

• Your rider(s) will feel that their contribution (e.g. discussing how the horse feels in the warming up) is valued by you and relevant to the decisions being made about the progression of the lesson.

You may think that too many questions (especially with beginner riders or those with little experience) may be inhibiting and the rider(s) will not have enough depth of knowledge or confidence to answer. However, I have found that the more you build questions and listening into your teaching, the easier your sessions become, because the riders begin to think, get involved and take responsibility for their actions.

Consider the following types of pupil:

• Riders who are arrogant and think they can ride will often not communicate with you easily or be prepared to work at the basics.

• Riders who think they are great and talk down to you with a manner of 'What can you teach me that I don't already know?'

In both these cases the rider is usually so wrapped up in 'ME' that they have little or no empathy with the horse. The horse may then suffer; he ends up somewhere in the 'blame cycle', usually in the line before or after you and the rider is still *not responsible*!

Unless I am successful in encouraging these types of rider to 'self analyse' and consider their own commitment to the relationship between coach and athlete, I will ease myself out of the situation and avoid teaching them.

Some of you reading this book will not be in a position where you can make that choice; you may be in a school or college where you have no choice as to whether or not to teach your pupils. I hope that by introducing some of the questioning strategies mentioned you can at least make your selfish rider think of the others involved in the coaching/learning cycle and see that the most success will be achieved by *joint effort and responsibility*.

Joint responsibility to the horse

As equestrian sport coaches we have the added dimension of considering the horse. While we may at times put greater emphasis on the rider and then concentrate at other times more on the horse, it is really impossible to separate the two and treat them independently. We have a joint responsibility (with the rider) to the horse at all times. He is (or should be) a willing participant, but he is not a *volunteer*. We introduce him to the activity as a result of his breeding or selection. In the vast majority of cases he becomes a willing and enthusiastic partner, and in my experience, school horses and competition horses alike generally fulfil their role with consistent compliance and often obvious enjoyment. The horse is, however, an animal and we must not forget that. The rider/coach responsibility to the horse is:

• To be consistent in every aspect of handling and training him.

• To remember his nature and instinctive behaviour and ensure that the way we 'train' him links into that.

• To reward and encourage him and ensure that when problems arise steps are retraced to reconfirm understanding and confidence.

• To continually assess the horse's ability and understanding of the work being expected of him, and adjust or realign goals if the horse shows limitations.

In summary: rider and coach should work together for the good of the horse.

The partnership between rider, horse and coach

For the coach this can be an exciting and stimulating relationship. I would have to say that in more than 30 years in the business it is still the reason I get 'a buzz', and it motivates me to explore every avenue to improve the ability or success of the riders I train.

It is a constantly evolving relationship that changes steadily because of the factors we will now consider:

• When you take on a new partnership to coach you are finding out about them and likewise they are finding out about you.

• The joint responsibility for the rider's progress begins, aims and goals are discussed and a plan is set out for their achievement.

• Many factors must be taken into account (e.g. age, stage of training and fitness of the horse, ability of the rider, time rider has to train, amount of training rider can undertake, expectations or aims of the rider, etc. – the list is endless!)

• Success will develop the partnership and while failure may cause its demise, more hopefully it may produce a major change in direction (e.g. to concentrate more on one aspect of the training which has shown up as a weakness; the possible review of suitability of the horse for the role; the consideration of other strategies for dealing with specific issues such as nerves prior to competition, etc.).

As mentioned in Chapter 3, your greatest achievement as a coach should be to empower your rider to go out and perform to his/her maximum level of ability, with minimum or no input from you.

Inevitably, sometimes your riders will 'move on'. Riders progress in their competence and confidence and may need to move on to progress further. This is not in any way a negative reflection on the coaching that you have given them – if anything, the opposite. If you have played a successful part in a rider's development then this can never be changed. Even if they go on to world-class achievement, *you* will know that you started them on the road to their success, or helped them at some stage along it. Personally you can harbour the satisfaction that your motivation and coaching techniques gave them a foundation for their future success.

SUMMARY

CHAPTER 5

■ QUESTIONS ESTABLISH THE RELATIONSHIP BETWEEN COACH AND RIDER.

■ LEARNING IS ONLY ACHIEVED THROUGH A JOINT COMMITMENT FROM COACH AND PUPIL.

■ AGREED AIMS FOR ANY SESSION WILL ENSURE THAT EXPECTATIONS FOR BOTH RIDER AND COACH ARE MET.

■ ONGOING REVIEW OF WORK WITHIN A SESSION WILL ENABLE THE RIDER TO BE FULLY INVOLVED IN THEIR COMMITMENT TO THE SUCCESS OF A SESSION.

■ AWARENESS OF RIDER AND COACH OF THE HORSE'S WELL-BEING AND UNDERSTANDING OF THE WORK ARE FUNDAMENTAL IN THE JOINT RELATIONSHIP BETWEEN HORSE, RIDER AND COACH.

TOP TIPS TOP TIPS TOP TIPS TOP TIPS

■ Agree with your rider what are realistic and appropriate aims for a session.

■ Hand over responsibility for the outcome of a lesson to the rider, then assist them in achieving the aim.

■ ALWAYS remember that the horse is a horse; he does not have reasoning power and in general does not have human thoughts, emotions and aspirations.

AIMS

AN AIM IS AN OBJECT OR PURPOSE THAT WE ARE ENDEAVOURING TO ACHIEVE. WHEN WE AIM AT SOMETHING WE IMMEDIATELY HAVE A DIRECTION. LET US THINK ABOUT WHAT AIMS A RIDER MIGHT HAVE AND HOW THESE ARE CONSIDERED AND WORKED ON BY THE COACH.

When helping a rider to set 'aims' (towards a goal or objective) we must first be able to assess the rider and their horse (the partnership). From this assessment the direction can be set and the speed of achievement can be considered. It sounds very simple but, of course, there will be any number of variables that may knock the basic direction off course – e.g. fitness of horse/rider, changing circumstances not initially visible when the aim was first considered and set. For this reason, aims must be:

+ Negotiable, flexible and adjustable.
+ Considered in the short, medium and long-term views.
+ Re-assessed on a regular basis.
+ Achievable and realistic (appropriate to the individual).
+ Agreed by rider and coach, with a time-span.
+ Interesting and stimulating to the rider, so that he or she feels motivated by the goal.
+ Adjusted when a goal is achieved, to set a new focus. Note the variable nature of an aim. It may be very small and only pertinent to one particular lesson (e.g. jumping a cross-pole for the first time) – this would be a short-term goal. It may be a much larger goal with a bigger vision (e.g. to be selected for a national team). The latter

would be a long-term aim and by its very specific and demanding nature it must have smaller, achievable 'stepping-stone' goals along the way, so that satisfaction and motivation are maintained towards the ultimate goal. Additionally, of course, these small 'stepping stones' are also 'building blocks' – in addition to their psychological benefit, they are enhancing actual performance.

Planning

Once we start to consider aims, our thoughts are drawn to the idea of planning. This, in my view, is an essential element of coaching that is relevant to all aspects, from a single lesson (or even part of one) right across the spectrum to helping a rider prepare for international competition.

Referring to the 'single lesson' scenario, coaches often say to me, 'I just respond to what I see happening as it happens and then the teaching is always appropriate to the needs of the pupil(s) on that occasion'. I can see the argument for this and acknowledge that it prevents the situation of preparing and giving a pre-planned, stereotyped lesson that is 'technically' a 'competent' lesson but actually fails to serve the needs of the pupil(s). But this leads us to consider further:

- **What, truly, is a competent lesson?**

We could start off by saying, quite correctly, that it is:

✦   A session that is safe for all participants (horses, riders, coach, other observers of the lesson).

✦   A lesson that is clear and easily understood by the pupil(s).

✦   A lesson that is technically delivering sound information and good practice.

✦   A lesson that is progressive and absorbed by the pupil(s) without loss of competence or confidence.

But, to these worthwhile criteria we should add:

✦   A lesson that fulfils the needs of the pupil(s).

✦   A lesson that is interesting, fun, challenging, stimulating, and satisfying. (I am sure you can add some more criteria to this list, which is certainly not exhaustive.)

It is true that an experienced coach will often be capable of delivering very competent sessions without prior planning. (Although, very often, if you ask some questions of an experienced coach who says – or even thinks – that they don't plan, you discover that, in fact, *there was some planning* in almost every case. The coach was just so experienced that the planning was *automatic*.) However, sooner or later without planning (of some kind) a session will be vulnerable to possible inadequacies that planning would avoid. There is a very real risk that, without *planning and thought* given prior to the delivery of coaching, failure to meet the needs of the pupil(s) is much more likely and this, in turn, can lead to many negative outcomes for both pupil(s) and coach.

Course-walking; one of many important aspects of planning.

To take the simple example of a single lesson, planning ensures that:

✦ You know how many riders you are working with.
✦ You are aware of the facilities that you will have to teach in (indoors, outdoors, artificial surface, grass.)
✦ You know how long a session you will be delivering.
✦ You have sufficient work to cover within the time.
✦ You will satisfy the requirements of the rider(s).

While you might manage a one-off session without due regard for these criteria, it is unlikely that you would be able to deliver a worthwhile programme of lessons without planning.

How to plan

If you are going on a journey where you know the point of origin and the point of destination, to be successful in reaching the latter it will be a great help if you study a map and plan the route! I know you are telling me that you have 'Sat Nav' but, believe me, the computer still has to calculate the journey and it is unable to do this unless you give it sufficient information!

Consider the pupil(s) whom you teach as wanting to make a journey. Whether that journey is from:

(a) *Unconscious incompetence* (total beginner, never having ridden) to *conscious incompetence* (able to control a trained horse in walk, trot and canter).

Or:

(b) Competing at national level to aiming for international level.

The planning can follow the same process in each rider's case.

1. *Identify* the rider's needs.

2. Coach and rider must *communicate*. Especially with bigger aims, this will often be with a 'heart to heart' discussion that may have other people of influence present (parents, if rider is a child – partner if rider is an adult).

3. The *route* to the end of the journey (aim) is the outcome of the discussion. The 'journey' will have an end destination (whether major competition at the end of the season, or improved canter transition for that single lesson 'today').

Even in a weekly class lesson, consideration must still be given to a short journey (plan for 45- or 60-minute riding session): what can be covered and how it is achieved. Thus the plan may be a short-term plan with a short-term outcome (or aim) or it may be a much bigger long term-plan with many smaller 'goals' along the route.

Good planning requires:

✦ The coach to be *organised* so that each training session is a step towards a bigger 'goal' rather than an isolated event that may or may not achieve progress.

✦ The coach and pupil(s) to agree a timescale for setting small goals and larger goals as markers along the route to the planned destination.

✦ The coach to be able to review progress and either accelerate the progress to marker goals, or adapt to readjust a goal that is not going to be achievable because of unforeseen circumstances (e.g. lameness of horse, rider having work/school commitments that inhibit the riding programme).

Good planning:

✦ Helps to maintain motivation (see later).
✦ Ensures that the progress is measurable and identifiable.

Assessment

- *What does assessment mean?*
- *For a coach, why is it necessary to assess?*
- *How do you assess, and how frequently?*

To assess means to make an estimate or judgement. In the coach's case this would be to estimate a horse's and rider's ability (both singly and as a partnership), and to consider existing expertise (or lack of it) and give judgement. Following assessment, it is then possible to consider a plan or programme for development.

✦   Assessing is therefore a very fundamental tool of the coach.

✦   Assessment is almost certainly ongoing in every teaching situation and becomes automatic to the experienced coach.

✦   Assessment becomes closely allied and linked to judgement, which we have already discussed in Chapter 4.

✦   Assessment will ensure that the risk consideration in any session is also ongoing.

✦   Assessment confirms existing knowledge, ensures ongoing understanding and, at the end of a session, ensures that the understanding is maintained.

Methods for assessing

- Where riders are concerned, the most familiar method for assessing would be *observation of practical 'doing'*. To decide on existing ability you would watch your rider(s) through a series of exercises or work that had been agreed between you.

- *Questions* will tell you a great deal, not only about your rider's knowledge but also their enthusiasm, motivation and interest in the lesson.

• Occasionally, asking for a written opinion might also reveal information about your pupils that had not come to light before. (A rider may not be very co-ordinated and thus find the 'doing' quite difficult but be extremely knowledgeable about what they are 'trying' to do.)

• With competing riders, competition results and factors such as ability to establish partnerships with unfamiliar horses would be significant.

• Remember that your assessment will depend on many outside factors, all of which will come into your consideration of the 'risk factor' – examples being: individual rider or a group? If a group, how many? Facilities? Influences such as weather, ground, etc.

Get into the habit of 'continually assessing', then nothing is left to chance and your judgement of how to develop a lesson is *always* supported by your assessment.

Evaluation

Another role of the coach is to continually assess, plan and *evaluate*.

• *So what is evaluation and why is it a vital tool of coaching?*

Evaluating from a coaching perspective is considering the existing standard or competence of a horse/rider combination and then, as a result of this evaluation, planning further training.

How does a coach evaluate?

+ Through observation.
+ Through questioning.
+ Through a rider's competence and results in competition.
+ Perhaps through other aspects, such as assessing the rider's ability in riding other horses.

Development

• *What is development?*

• *How do you develop a lesson?*

• *How do you decide which exercises and what work to do within a lesson?*

Development can be described as:

+ A gradual unfolding or growth.
+ Bringing to a higher or more advanced state.
+ Bringing out what is latent, or potential.
+ Evolving.

Our aim as a coach should always be to *develop* the rider's skill, knowledge, and understanding and therefore enhance their ability.

How to develop the rider and *what* work to choose to ensure that development occurs is dependent on the coach's skill.

An astute coach will use various methods to develop a rider's skill – here, modern technology in the form of a mechanical horse.

We have already discussed some of the coach's tools: *communication, awareness,* and *assessment;* all are vital and relevant to the choices you then make for the rider's development.

In general, development must be:

• Split up into manageable 'chunks' of work that the rider can understand and carry out and that the horse is physically and mentally capable of doing.

• Progressive, and move clearly through stages of understanding for both rider and horse.

• Appropriate to the learning style of the rider.

• Adaptable to the circumstances of a specific occasion. (For example: a choice of some particular work on a warm, sunny day outside may be very different from that on a cold winter's day when the wind is blowing sharply around the arena.)

• Easily identified and agreed by the rider as being a progressive pathway with which the rider feels comfortable.

The way you might develop a group lesson of four to six riders would be different from the way you would develop the work for an individual rider, even though the skill levels of the group and the individual were the same.

In choosing the method for development (e.g. working towards some lateral movements with riders competing at Elementary level) it is important that you constantly review the progress that you are making. Let us consider two scenarios:

Scenario 1

Scenario 1: Four riders on their own horses in a Riding Club clinic; riders are all competing at Novice/Elementary level; all horses are between 6 and 16 years old. You have not taught any of these riders before.

The suggested lesson plan might be:

• Introduce yourself and find out the riders' names, how long they have had their horses, how often they ride/school, what they consider to be their personal strengths and weaknesses, what (if anything) worries them?

• *Agreed aim: to work in walk, trot and canter and develop some lateral work.*

• A warm-up session would then begin, with you continuing to find out information at random (e.g. have the riders ridden in this venue before, how often do they have training, etc.).

• The warm-up progresses very calmly, with all riders well in control and the horses working quietly as a group.

• The warm-up would include some stretching and suppling work (for horse and rider). During this time you would be making an assessment of each horse and rider, beginning to accumulate information from which you will choose the way the lesson develops and what work you will actually use to help produce improvement.

• If all riders and their horses show a reasonable degree of basic competence and control in the working-in (in open order) and this produces a clear loosening effect, you might go on to work more specifically on transitions both between and within the gaits.

• During this important warming-up phase, ongoing questions will ensure that you maintain an awareness of how your riders feel. Your riders should also gain confidence in their communication and rapport with you and this, in turn, leads to increased relaxation.

• By the time the ride have worked for 10 to 15 minutes you should have the following information:

    ✦ A clear picture of how each rider sits; their balance, suppleness and co-ordination.

    ✦ An awareness of the quality of each horse's basic gaits.

    ✦ An awareness of the general attitude of each horse (sharp, lazy, stiff, loose).

    ✦ A fairly clear picture of how hard each rider works for themselves.

    ✦ An idea of how well the riders communicate with you and their awareness of how the horse is going underneath them.

    ✦ A confident plan of how you might develop the lesson based on the above assessment.

The lesson may then progress in a number of ways; perhaps any of the following choices could be appropriate:

✦ Leg-yield in walk and then trot.
✦ Turns on the forehand and then some walk-to-canter transitions.
✦ Work without stirrups, concentrating on rider position and feel.
✦ Riding on the 'inner track', working on transitions, to improve the riders' awareness of 'straightness'.
✦ Some shortening and lengthening of the trot and canter.

The list of choices is wide and largely dependent on the coach's experience and depth of knowledge for ideas and exercises.

Scenario 2

Scenario 2: Group of four riders mounted on their own horses; all horses between 6 and 16 years old. These are Riding Club members competing at Novice/Elementary level. You have not taught these riders before.

You start the lesson in exactly the same way as Scenario 1.

• The riders start to warm up in open order, and from a very early stage it is evident that one horse is tense and anxious and his rider is equally ill at ease.

• Very quickly the anxiety affects one or two others in the group and the horses begin to behave in a sharp and unpredictable way.

• At this point, questions will only distract the riders more and increase the tension of an already tense situation.

• It is necessary for you to intervene and 'take control' of a deteriorating situation.

• You may need to put all the horses on the same rein; you may need to bring them back to walk, or even to put them into a single file ride order with at least one horse's length between them to gain control and reinstate confidence.

• This may take some time and may necessitate you working for a while in walk only.

- Your lesson plan would need to be completely adjusted to take into account the circumstances that arose on this occasion.

- It is almost impossible to completely pre-plan a lesson, especially with riders you do not know.

- It is imperative that you always consider what is happening 'today' and make your choices and plan for development based primarily on that assessment.

While the above two scenarios *started* in the same way, the *outcome* of the lesson would be entirely dependent on the choices you made for each of the circumstances that arose.

Outcomes

- *What is an outcome? Or is it THE outcome?*

- *Is the outcome inevitable or predictable?*

- *Is the outcome guaranteed?*

- *Is it always an expected or good outcome?*

If there is an aim then there should be an *outcome*, because *an* outcome or the outcome is the *consequence* or *result* of something. In planning a lesson you almost certainly have an idea of the outcome that you are aiming for. The aim of the lesson (depending on the competence of the rider(s)) will be discussed and agreed between rider(s) and coach.

Whether that outcome is assured depends on many things. It may depend on some of the following:

- ✦   The competence of the rider.
- ✦   The competence, judgement and guidance of the coach.
- ✦   The co-operation of the horse.

✦   The surrounding conditions (e.g. ground, weather, outside influences).

✦   The motivation and effort/commitment of the rider.

✦   The time available.

Satisfaction

Satisfaction is a great motivator. Reaching an aim or goal gives a great sense of achievement and a sense of self-worth, which often drives the person to strive harder for the next goal. Ironically, however, consistent and regular achievement and satisfaction can have a 'down side', in that it can allow riders to slip into a state of complacency and *de-motivation*. They become 'comfortable' in their regular success and inadvertently stop trying so hard. This can easily become a dangerous, slippery slope and it is the coach's duty to ensure that this does not happen. Aims and goals must be assessed on an ongoing basis and adjusted as necessary to maintain motivation.

Of course, safeguarding against complacent reactions does not mean that satisfaction should ever be considered a 'bad' thing and, ideally, a satisfactory outcome would be achieved for all aims. However, in an imperfect world this is not always possible, for some of the reasons already given.

On the occasions when the rider does not achieve a sense of satisfaction after a lesson this must be recognised by the coach.

• In some cases, a lack of satisfaction can be turned into a *motivator* for future work.

• The coach must be quick to adjust the direction of a lesson if the rider is showing dissatisfaction (see scenario below).

• The coach must be able to discuss the feelings of the rider towards the loss of achievement/satisfaction. (For example, the rider may be getting tired.) Then a potentially negative situation can be usefully turned around into a learning situation or a motivator for future occasions.

• The coach, in conjunction with the rider (depending on their standard), should adjust the intensity of the work/exercise if it is proving too difficult for the horse and thus causing a lack of achievement and satisfaction.

Scenario

Consider the following scenario: This rider has her own competition horse with whom she is very comfortable and familiar.

• She regularly takes private lessons with her coach, whom she knows well.

• Her horse is genuine and usually jumps clear rounds in show jumping.

• This rider wins a lot of ribbons on the basis of the horse being careful, and the rider now *expects* him to go clear.

• The rider has moved up a class and is jumping slightly bigger tracks. The horse is tending to collect four faults from time to time and this is becoming costly.

• The rider's attitude is that the horse has become careless. She is irritated by her slight loss of form.

• The rider's state of mind at the beginning of the lesson is one of blaming the faults that she has begun to have on the horse.

• The coach must discuss the situation with the rider and use work which demonstrates to the rider how cleanly the horse jumps as a rule: a grid with some short distances to encourage the horse to be quicker to adjust his stride and be neat in front.

• The rider needs to be encouraged to take responsibility for her horse's 'loss of form'.

• She must consider the type of fence (if there is a pattern) he has down – is it a vertical, or in a combination? Does it follow an oxer? Is it off one particular rein?

• If the rider is encouraged to consider where the fault(s) occurs, then she can take some responsibility for how she rides that fence;

the turn, the balance, the quality of the canter, etc. and then play a part in the *outcome*.

• The rider is directed both by the coach's approach and by the work chosen to take on the responsibility for the horse herself. In this way the rider is 'in control' of the *outcome*.

In such a situation it is all too common that the coach shoulders all the responsibility, allowing the rider to stay in her state of complacency of blaming the horse. In such a case, the *outcome* of the lesson would not be *satisfaction* and the fault would perpetuate.

When the aim and the outcome are incompatible

There will be occasions when the rider's *aim* is unrealistic, either in the time-span allowed, or relating to the ability of either horse or rider (see also Expectations in Chapter 10). There will also be occasions (sometimes unexpected and unpredicted) when the *outcome* is totally incompatible with the *aim*.

It is your responsibility as an experienced coach to try to minimise the occasions when this happens. Let's look at how this can be achieved.

Guiding the rider to an appropriate aim

Points for consideration are:

+ The time allowed.
+ The capability of horse and rider.
+ The facilities available (including the risk assessment).

Scenario 1

Scenario 1

• Young child rider, Jimmy (own pony), attends a group clinic aimed at 'dressage training'.

- Coach asks the rider what he would like to do today.

- 'I want to jump,' is the reply.

- There is not a jump in sight (all other riders are sitting on dressage saddles!).

Either:

- You say, 'We can't jump today, we are doing dressage.'
This instantly de-motivates the child, especially as YOU had asked what he wanted to do!

Or:

- You can say, 'Although there are no jumps here we can use some poles on the ground. This will help your control and accuracy, and Jimmy you can work in a forward position. This will help your balance for another time when there are some jumps available.'
    This keeps the rider who had hoped to jump feeling positive that he is working towards something that is going to help his jumping 'next time'.

Scenario 2

Scenario 2

- Here we have a private lesson with a rider on her own horse. The horse is a Thoroughbred known to get tense. The rider then also becomes tense and the partnership loses harmony.

- The agreed aim is to work on reducing tension as there is a competition this weekend.

- Lesson is progressing very well and then a commotion outside the school just before the end causes the horse to lose attention and the resulting tension upsets both horse and rider.

- Rider grabs hold of the horse and gets tearful, saying the whole lesson has been a waste of time.

Either:

• Agree with the rider and send her home 'in bits'!

Or:

• Spend the last five or ten minutes in walk defusing the situation, by encouraging the rider to accept that the horse may easily lose attention and she must develop a 'strategy' for managing it.

• Discuss the rider's ability to 'feel' the tension creeping in and being able to 'read' a situation *before* it happens, and try to move away to an area of the showground with more space and calm.

• Encourage the rider to maintain her own self-control so that she continues to instil calm and consistency in the horse.

• Encourage the rider to return to walk (sometimes on a long rein) even if it is only minutes before they are due to compete.

Be able to discuss with your pupil(s) either after a lesson or as a result of competing:

✦   What their aim was.

✦   Whether that aim was achieved.

✦   If so, what is their next aim?

✦   If not, why not, and what adjustments can they make to realign the aim and make it achievable?

✦   If the outcome and the aim were totally incompatible, what circumstances arose which changed the intended outcome, and was the aim appropriate at the start?

It is essential that *aims* and *outcomes* are constantly considered, reviewed and adjusted as a means of *motivating* and achieving *satisfaction*.

SUMMARY

■ AIMS ARE ESSENTIAL FOR GIVING THE RIDER OBJECTIVES TO WORK TOWARDS.

■ PLANNING HELPS TO PROVIDE A 'MAP' THAT INDICATES A VIABLE ROUTE FROM THE AIM TO THE OBJECTIVE.

■ IT IS THE COACH'S RESPONSIBILITY TO ASSESS, AND THIS ENSURES ONGOING APPROPRIATE CHOICE OF WORK FOR HORSE AND RIDER.

■ DEVELOPMENT BRINGS OUT THE POTENTIAL OF A HORSE/RIDER.

■ DEVELOPMENT MUST BE ADJUSTABLE WITH ASSESSMENT.

■ THE OUTCOME WILL IDEALLY LEAD TO SATISFACTION IN THE RIDER, WHICH IN TURN BUILDS CONFIDENCE AND SELF-ESTEEM.

TOP TIPS TOP TIPS TOP TIPS TOP TIPS

■ Make sure that aims are always realistic, achievable and flexible.

■ To reiterate a key point – assessment is about using your judgement; if in doubt, don't!

■ If the rider is feeling dissatisfied make sure that they take responsibility for the outcome and help them adjust it to re-motivate them or induce satisfaction.

COACH-LED AND RIDER-LED TRAINING

I HAVE PREVIOUSLY TOUCHED UPON THE CONCEPTS OF WORK BEING COACH-LED OR RIDER-LED; IN THIS CHAPTER I WANT TO EXPLORE THESE CONCEPTS IN MORE DETAIL AND RELATE THEM TO SITUATIONS IN WHICH YOU AS A COACH MIGHT FIND YOURSELF.

When a person comes to a sport with little or no background knowledge of it, it is absolutely essential for them to be fully informed about what they are trying to do. With horses it is of paramount importance, both for the rider's safety and for the welfare of the horse involved, that the instructor/coach takes full responsibility for the information given and the progress of the lesson. As the rider develops in knowledge and competence, confidence should naturally evolve, and with this confidence should come an increasing desire on the rider's part to take some control or initiative. This is the critical time when the coach must be able to recognise how much to relinquish 'control' and also be able to encourage the rider to develop self-reliance and independence.

How styles develop

In this chapter we will take some hypothetical scenarios and consider where the training would best benefit from a coach-led learning session and when a rider-led session would be the better choice.

Inevitably, there is some overlap and the experienced coach will show an aptitude for adapting from one style to another to best facilitate the learning of the pupil(s).

Scenario 1

Scenario 1: Child of ten has been given a course of six riding lessons for her birthday, having never ridden before and only seen ponies trekking while on holiday, or on television.

Here the 'rider' has little or no prior knowledge other than a visual idea of 'riding'. She may not ever have been close to a pony or had any experience of handling them. For safety, and to ensure that the child's first few experiences of contact with a pony are pleasant ones, the following *coach-led* training is essential.

• The child will need early advice about what to wear, including footwear, hat, suitable trousers/jeans, gloves and safe jacket/sweater.

• There will need to be some introduction relating to the size of the pony, the handling, approach, equipment (saddle, bridle, headcollar).

• It will help the child's confidence if she knows where she will be riding and who will be helping her, and how many (if any) other riders are likely to be there.

All this happens before the rider has even been shown how to mount the pony!

• The first lesson is likely to cover how to lead the pony, how to make the girth secure, how to run down stirrups and how to mount.

• This will be followed by how to sit, how to hold the reins and how to begin basic control of the pony.

- Small periods of controlled movement should follow; almost certainly the rider will be on a lead rein or a lunge rein.

- Information on 'stopping' and 'starting', turning left and right should be included in an early riding lesson.

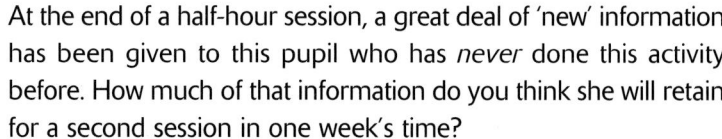

At the end of a half-hour session, a great deal of 'new' information has been given to this pupil who has *never* done this activity before. How much of that information do you think she will retain for a second session in one week's time?

Visually:
✦ She may remember seeing the pony led out to meet her.
✦ She may remember what colour the pony was.
✦ She may remember how big he looked when she got close to him.

Kinaesthetically:
✦ She may remember how nervous she felt.
✦ She may remember how thick the pony's coat felt when she patted him.
✦ She may remember how great it felt to first sit astride the pony.

Audibly:
✦ She may remember hearing his metal shoes on the concrete yard.

If you ask her to recount how to tighten the girth and the sequence of procedure for mounting, she may only remember one or two points other than the feeling of sitting in the saddle.

In the second and subsequent lessons you will need to reiterate much of the information that was covered in a first lesson. It may take several sessions or weeks before the first stage of *conscious competence* becomes apparent. This state of *conscious competence* will show itself at different stages with different riders. Some riders may be able to walk, trot and canter quite efficiently within a few lessons; other riders may take many more lessons and weeks or even months more time.

Conscious competence may be influenced or affected by:

✦ The rider's 'nerve' or courage.
✦ The rider's natural co-ordination and suppleness.
✦ The rider's natural balance.
✦ The rider's determination.
✦ The rider's innate talent/ability for riding (or any other sport).
✦ How much effort the rider puts in for himself or herself without only relying on you, the coach.

Scenario 2

Scenario 2: Girl of ten, has ridden with siblings since they were very small, at home with ponies they grew up on. Siblings' interests are moving into other areas, but this young girl has decided she wants lessons to 'be an eventer when she grows up'.

Here is a child who has been riding 'all her life'; she probably thinks she can ride (and to some degree, of course, she can). You, as the professional coach, may find many and huge gaps in her 'knowledge' although she may have quite a level of *unconscious competence!* She can probably walk, trot, canter and gallop! She can probably jump (and stay on!). The way in which you approach her as her instructor/coach can now encourage her to ensure that her knowledge of 'what she is doing' becomes more assured by knowing 'why she is doing it' and 'how she is doing it'. Conversely, if you try to 'control' the sessions in a totally coach-led way, it is quite likely that you will shut down the rider's natural flair and independence and you may run the risk of the rider stating that lessons are 'boring' because she can ride and they don't 'do enough' except learn 'theory'.

Your approach with the rider 'who can already ride' must be to encourage them to explore 'how well they ride' and how much they know about what they are doing and what effect it has on the horse.

In this case, you know that the rider has some ability and competence. It is up to you to assess that competence and still maintain a safe situation while discovering the level of knowledge.

The way you might develop a lesson for the child in this scenario might go something like this:

• Having chosen a pony you think is suitable, invite the rider to 'show you' how they lead the pony out, prepare to mount and mount up.

• At this stage, if there are large areas of procedure that indicate a lack of knowledge which could lead to a lack of safety (e.g. leading out with the stirrups dangling, or mounting without making the girth firm) your approach needs to be to ask, 'What would happen if…?' (for example, 'you mounted with the girth loose') rather than saying, 'Don't do this or that'.

• Always allow a rider to 'find out by experience' (as long as the experience does not put them in potential danger). In this way the rider will have a *kinaesthetic* learning experience, which tends to be more reinforcing than an *audible* 'don't do this' approach.

• Allow the lesson to evolve on a basis of, 'show me what you usually do, or what you can do'.

• *Question* at each stage of the work to assess the depth of knowledge or understanding from the child.

◆ Can you show me some work in trot on both reins?
◆ Can you ride 20 m circles?
◆ Can you make a transition from walk to trot and trot to walk?
◆ Was that a good transition and, if so, what made it good/bad?

At any stage, assess the rider's confidence in both what she is trying to do and in you. At any stage you can adapt your teaching style to lead the work more if you need to. (For example, if the rider is finding difficulty in going from trot to canter, you might structure some help to guide the rider when to ask for canter and what aids to use.)

At the end of a half-hour session with this child you should know in your opinion:

✦ How *unconsciously competent* she is.
✦ What her underpinning knowledge is to support what she can do.
✦ How determined she is.
✦ How courageous she is.
✦ How hard she tries.
✦ How secure, co-ordinated and effective she is.

As a result of this session you should then be able to plan in your mind what programme of work you would devise for this rider to:

• Stimulate her enthusiasm to find out more about what she could do, so that she could do it better with more knowledge.

• Maintain her self-confidence and self-esteem in her existing competence but begin a commitment to further improvement through the expertise you can offer as her coach.

• Believe that she is quite good and therefore how much better she could be with some good coaching (from you).

Changing emphasis

If you are coaching with awareness there should be a subtle change in your 'management' of lessons (class or individual) from the work being coach-led to rider-led, or back again, depending upon circumstance.

We have seen that lessons need to be totally coach-led if dealing with beginners or riders lacking knowledge and confidence, but starting with, or switching to, this strategy may also be necessary:

• If riders are learning new work or needing to consolidate work which needs revision, and you the coach can introduce specific exercises to work on that specific aspect of work.

- If the horse is being difficult and confidence is being lost (then the coach may take an 'upper hand').

- If the situation (from a safety angle) dictates that the coach takes the lead or authority. (For example, in a group where riders are all working independently but one rider falls off and the coach instantly takes control of the ride to stop them all and deal with the incident.)

- Any other unforeseen circumstance where the coach must have the ultimate authority over the individual or group.

If that ultimate authority of coach over pupil is lost then the relationship between coach and pupil is probably coming to a conclusion.

An example of a coach-led session – in this case, dictated by the nature of the lesson, in which the rider is being lunged without reins.

In a rider-led session, the rider may suggest issues that require coaching input

Keeping the balance

In my opinion the key to keeping the balance between the coach-led session and the rider-led session is COMMUNICATION.

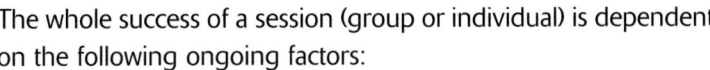

The whole success of a session (group or individual) is dependent on the following ongoing factors:

✦ Assessment.
✦ Awareness throughout, reading the evolving work and observing its success or otherwise.
✦ Communication with the rider(s) to know what they are feeling and what is working (or not).
✦ More assessment.
✦ More awareness and communication.
✦ Knowing when to 'peak'; how much to ask of horse(s) and rider(s).
✦ Discussing how to progress and at what point to stop and 'leave it for another time'.

The more experienced your riders and the more involved they are with their horses the more you must liaise with them to agree the way forward. It is never 'giving in to them' to be guided by what they are feeling.

The more they work with their own horses the more you must discuss with them at the beginning and several times through a session 'how it is feeling for them'. You are the 'eyes' on the ground and the expertise that hopefully provides them with the exercises and work plan that will take their level of ability forward. The ongoing relationship between you and your pupils is dependent on good communication and your ability to draw out your pupils' personality and confidence. You may have to act as friend, counsellor, shoulder to cry on, motivator, go-between, teacher and manager –and be prepared to act as a good groom!

One final aspect of striking the balance between coach-led and rider-led sessions comes down to the simple fact that we are all human and subject to changes of mood. On some days a rider may be very self-motivated and the direction of a session may be largely rider-led. On another day, the rider may be looking for much more leading from you. You must learn to be adaptable and having 'read' the situation, be able to act accordingly.

SUMMARY

■ COACH-LED WORK WILL TEND TO BE MORE APPROPRIATE FOR LESS EXPERIENCED OR KNOWLEDGEABLE RIDERS.

■ RIDER-LED SESSIONS TEND TO DEVELOP AS THE RIDER BECOMES MORE SELF-SUFFICIENT.

■ YOU, AS A COACH, MUST BE ADAPTABLE AND BE ABLE TO MOVE FROM A COACH-LED TEACHING STYLE TO A RIDER-LED SESSION WITH EASE.

■ IF IN DOUBT, COMMUNICATION WITH YOUR RIDER IS USUALLY A KEY TO ESTABLISHING THE BALANCE BETWEEN COACH-LED AND RIDER-LED WORK.

■ ASSESSMENT, AWARENESS, JUDGEMENT AND COMMUNICATION ARE KEY FACTORS IN GETTING THE BALANCE RIGHT BETWEEN COACH-LED AND RIDER-LED WORK.

TOP TIPS TOP TIPS TOP TIPS TOP TIPS

■ Listen to what your riders are telling you – this always helps in making decisions.

■ Don't be afraid to be flexible in your teaching: sometimes allow the rider to lead a session; sometimes take control if circumstances dictate that you should do so.

COACHING CHILDREN

TO BE INVOLVED IN THE INTRODUCTION OF ANY CHILD TO SPORT OF ANY KIND IS EXCITING, CHALLENGING AND BOTH A PRIVILEGE AND A RESPONSIBILITY.

The way in which a child receives early initiation into a sport can prove a lifelong influence on that child's attitude to that sport – and, in some cases, to sport in general.

A child approaches a new activity (be it sport or any other challenge of life of which they have no prior experience) with an innocence and total lack of expectation or preconceived ideas. It is past experience – whether good or bad – that may mould opinion and attitude for the future. Without this, a child comes to the sport with an openness and innocence that puts a huge responsibility on you, the coach, to ensure that their first and ongoing impressions of the activity stimulate and motivate them to further participation.

Starting age and motivation

- Is there an ideal age at which a child should begin to learn to ride?

There will be many opinions on the answer to this question. A child who is born into a 'horsy' family is likely to have very early initiation into horses purely because they are 'part of the family'. Involvement with horses in this way is perfect. Just as a child who grows up in the snowy slopes of Switzerland is likely to be able to ski as easily as he or she runs about, so will a child who grows up with horses in the family be 'able to ride' without remembering their early introduction and the act of 'learning' the skill.

For the child who is not so fortunate other factors may be important and relevant:

+ Why does the child want to ride?
+ What opportunity is there in close proximity to home?
+ Will the riding opportunity be formal and structured (professional teaching) or 'having a go on a friend's pony'?
+ Is the child physically well developed and positive or small and nervous in disposition?

From my experience both of teaching children for many years and from running a riding school (also for many years), the following general criteria will direct a child rider towards a successful and happy relationship in riding as their chosen sport.

• The child *must want* to ride. The interest must not only be from the parents, who may want their child to ride for many other reasons. (Want their child to have an opportunity that they missed out on; feel that socially it is something their child should be able to do; they themselves rode and think their child should too, etc.)

• The child must *enjoy* being around horses and ponies. If the child doesn't like getting dirty, wet or cold then riding is not the sport for them.

• The child needs to be physically developed enough to be able to manage a pony, to lead, mount, dismount and begin basic walk and trot work (with help).

• The child needs to be old enough to maintain short bouts of concentration for developing basic technical skill.

● The child may be apprehensive and need encouragement to become more confident, but if they are genuinely scared of riding (which usually shows very early on) then in my opinion riding is not the sport for them.

● Although small children can be usefully led around on horseback, which will familiarise them with the animal, formal 'training' will probably be most effective to start broadly between the ages of 4 and 7.

Enjoyment is a fundamental requirement – children having fun on ponies.

Referring back to the first point above, my young instructors would sometimes say to me, 'But the parents insist the child must ride'. It is difficult to turn away business and, as a young instructor, it is often very hard to broach the subject with an assertive parent who is 'paying'. However, riding is a 'risk sport' and it is essential that there is willing participation from the rider. While riding school ponies and horses are, by the very nature of the job they are required to do, usually absolute paragons of virtue, they are still very much living and feeling animals and tense, nervous and frightened riders will sometimes induce anxiety and unpredictable reactions from them. Therefore, in the interests of the safety and welfare of both their pupils and horses, young instructors must develop the skill to advise parents of the wisdom or otherwise of insisting their child learns a sport to which they are not committed.

Physical considerations

All forms of sport for children should be enjoyable and therefore add to the quality of the child's life. Physical effort, particularly in young people who are still very much developing, must be encouraged in such a way that the muscles, ligaments and bones of the untrained child are strengthened gradually and not overstretched for short-term benefit which has a detrimental long-term effect. Fortunately, in equestrian sport, this is rarely the case but identification of the following may be relevant:

✦ Ensure that the pony/horse is not too wide for a slightly built rider.

✦ Ensure that the pony/horse is not too strong for the rider's security of position and they then feel a need to 'pull'.

✦ Ensure that a rider does not get physically or mentally tired.

✦ Learn to recognise signs of 'not coping'. (Switching off and not 'trying', losing confidence and doubting themselves reflected in frustration, losing aid co-ordination, anxiety or irritation when 'the horse won't do it', or 'I can't do it'.)

✦ Ensure that the rider has frequent breaks in the effort required, especially if riding is the only activity that the person takes in a week. (Not a whole hour's lesson without stirrups!)

✦ Ensure that the rider does not get cold, tired or wet in a session and direct the rider to put on a coat in relevant circumstances even if they insist there is no need.

✦ Ensure that in hot weather the rider has appropriate and regular re-hydration. (Water should be available to riders throughout a lesson.)

✦ If a rider has suffered any kind of injury that will interfere with performance, ensure that they do not ride again until the injury is repaired. (If the injury occurs during a riding session then appropriate action must be taken to help the rider and maintain relevant records afterwards.)

Teaching pointers

Children usually develop best when taught in groups. Teaching groups of children can be tremendous fun but is certainly challenging for the instructor. (I deliberately use the term 'instructor' here because with children you must be in control and for the most part with inexperienced child riders the session – especially a group session – will be *coach-led*. It is essential that the children respect you and will 'jump' when you say 'jump'. If you lose control then potentially the group may be unsafe.)

The following are some points to bear in mind when teaching children.

• Children will learn if they are *having fun* and *enjoying* themselves because the 'experience' is a good one.

• Children will develop and the experience will be good if they feel *safe*.

- Children need to feel *valued* – they will accept criticism as long as they do not feel victimised or belittled.

- You can challenge children and 'push them out of their comfort zone' as long as they have *confidence in you,* and you make them *believe in themselves.* ('If she thinks I can do it, then I must be able to.')

- Many children thrive in a competitive atmosphere and they will 'compete' against each other to be the 'best'. Remember that, when using this situation to further the work, you may still have some evolving *'reflectors'* and *'theorists'* who prefer to watch the *'activists'* being competitive while they learn by thinking about it or wanting to know more of the 'how to do it'.

How often should children ride?

It is very easy to state that the more often an activity is practised the more competent the practitioner becomes in the skill. It is also known that a skill that is established and developed as a child is a skill that becomes more 'automatic' into adulthood, even if that skill is lapsed for a while and then re-established.

Therefore, children should ride as often as time, finance and opportunity allow – as long as they 'want to'. Ideally, they should be involved in a range of sporting activities to develop all-round co-ordination and athleticism: this will be beneficial *whatever* their main sporting focus becomes.

In the early childhood years, riding may be the all-consuming passion but then, as adolescence approaches, it may be overwhelmed by other interests. For many people, riding becomes a 'background' skill (along with activities such as swimming, dancing, playing hockey or tennis) – something they did as a child – and perhaps they only revisit it years later when married and with children they 'go on a trekking holiday in Peru'.

Exceptionally talented child riders

To find that you are teaching a child who has exceptional talent is extremely exciting for any coach, but what identifies an *exceptionally talented rider*?

✦   A rider with exceptional ability or aptitude compared to other riders of a similar age or experience.

✦   A rider who finds the development of their riding skills easy and therefore makes abnormally fast progress.

✦   A rider who shows an outstanding commitment to their progress and development.

✦   An innate drive to be better; a rider who has an inner drive to be 'best'. (Note that real 'perfectionists' are internally driven to eliminate *all* flaws in their performance, with the result that they may put intense pressure on themselves.)

Developing talent

I was asked some years ago to give a talk to students who were studying for a Sports Coaching Degree. My subject was training elite youngsters in dressage. At the end of the talk, one of the students said that she felt 'It was wrong to pressurise these very young children (twelve to sixteen years) to such high achievement' (European Championship level). My immediate response was: 'No way are these youngsters put under any pressure from anyone, other than themselves.' All we do is support them in their aim and protect them from as much pressure as we can by making the pathway to their aim as straightforward as possible. In my experience, the thing that really sets apart a talented rider is their single-mindedness to achieve and often their total and utter commitment to their aim, to the point that everything else takes second place.

Roles of the parties involved

Often the biggest inhibitors of a talented child's development are the parents but – and it is a very big BUT – the parents are also more often than not the biggest support system, too.

The coach is in a unique position: he or she must be able to balance the role they play in the child's life as their talent evolves, while helping the parents to allow the child to develop as an athlete and grow away from being 'their precious little girl/boy'. That is probably one of the more difficult challenges for the coach of a talented rider.

Let us consider the evolution of the personalities concerned.

The talented child rider:

• Is prodigiously talented.

• Has a developing awareness of their own ability and, on achieving success, begins to thrive on winning and aims for more.

• With the support of the coach, begins to follow a plan for short/medium and long-term goals.

• Becomes aware of moving away from their peer group in terms of ability and seeks to maintain that status more and more.

• In turn this puts increased pressure on them, particularly at competitions.

• Sees and seeks a need for more intensive training.

The talented rider's coach:

• Recognises the ability and is enthused and excited to nurture and develop it.

• Becomes more focused on the all-round needs of the rider and begins to structure the short/medium and long-term goals.

• By virtue of the increased demands of coaching becomes more emotionally involved with the whole family through more familiarisation.

• Uses professional knowledge and expertise to advise the rider on relevant support (physiotherapy, sport psychology, etc.)

• Advises parents as to how the rider should be developed and what opportunities exist.

The parents:

• Initially, if they are not from an equestrian background, they may be completely unaware of the ability their child is beginning to show.

• They begin to be more aware that the child is winning or achieving frequently.

• They begin to be aware of the congratulations of others (parents, judges, officials).

• They should be gaining knowledge from the coach as to the evolving talent of their offspring.

• As the realisation dawns that they have a talented child then hopefully wholehearted support follows.

• This support can be difficult to balance if:
  ✦   There are other siblings:
      (a) Who also ride but are less talented, **or**
      (b) Don't ride but are involved in other sports or activities.
  ✦   Finances are limited and the evolving talent needs ever more training/entries to competitions/training away at elite squads, etc.
  ✦   They have their own commitments to a business (which finances the horses) or their own horses (which usually have to go on hold for a while).
  ✦   They have limited funds and have to consider the implications of a hugely expensive sport with limited (if any) return on their investment, other than seeing their child

succeed and it being a life-changing experience for both them and the child.

● They have never had to visit the emotions that start to run when they are watching their child compete:

✦ Against other riders for a place on a National or British team.

Coaching an exceptionally talented child rider is a challenging responsibility – and also a great privilege.

✦   When their child does not achieve as high a mark 'today' as last week, but 'today' is a selection trial.

✦   When the pony/horse goes lame the day before a major competition or at the European Championships before the trot up.

✦   When they experience hostility from other parents who see their child as a 'threat' to a place for their own offspring.

The talented rider will be developing very rapidly not only as a rider but also as a personality and this again can be very hard for the parents to recognise and adapt to. As the child experiences success and failure he or she is learning to deal with life-changing situations, and this can complicate the relationship between rider, parents and coach. Sometimes, for example, the parents' response to a seemingly poor dressage mark may be very different from that the coach will adopt.

Scenario 1

Scenario 1

• Rider has won the last four dressage competitions ridden in.

• At the next competition, the rider is slightly casual in their approach, a little short-tempered with the coach, telling the coach that they have worked in enough and the horse is fine.

• Horse is a little sharp in the test (coach thinks he has not worked in enough) and the mark reflects the tension.

• Rider does not win and is not happy.

• Parents look at the mark and commiserate with the rider, telling her that the judge 'doesn't like her' and is 'mean' and the test was much better than that anyway.

• The coach tries to debrief the rider, aiming to encourage her to see that she engineered her own problems through not working in enough and being casual about expecting the winning outcome.

- Rider becomes aggressive, telling the coach that her mum and dad thought it was OK and the judge 'didn't like me'; 'it wasn't my fault'.

This situation is extremely negative for all concerned.

✦   The rider and coach are not agreeing how the working in should progress.

✦   The rider is not taking responsibility for her own working in, in agreement with the knowledge and expertise of the coach.

✦   The parents are undermining the opinion of the judge (which should be upheld in all circumstances) and helping the rider to make excuses for poor performance.

✦   The rider is avoiding taking responsibility and again will not agree or discuss with the coach the reasons for poor outcome.

The future relationship between rider, coach and parents is likely to be severely compromised if this type of situation continues. The rider must take responsibility for her own actions, using the expertise of her coach to support and guide her. The parents need to support the coach and encourage the child to look constructively at the opinion of the judge and how it was reached on this occasion.

Scenario 2

Scenario 2

- Rider has been very successful in her last three events, winning on her dressage score.

- At the next competition, which is a big occasion with a title at stake, the rider is well placed after the dressage and is optimistic about the cross-country, having walked it carefully and with much thought.

- Across country the partnership have a costly glance-off a corner and then have two down show jumping and finish well down the pack.

- The rider is terribly disappointed and very 'down'.

• Parents are very supportive, giving the rider space to 'punish herself'; coach waits for the right time to discuss the outcome.

• In due time the parents supported the rider, 'being there' for her to vent her frustration and disappointment on them without retaliating. (Only a parent can take that load sometimes!)

• In due time the coach was able to talk through with her pupil how the huge expectations she had were dashed and how she would deal with the feeling of failure and then what could be learnt from it.

The outcome of this huge disappointment (for all parties) was a steep learning curve and the opportunity for the rider to see what a fine line there is between success and failure – and that both are going to happen. The lessons learnt from failure can hopefully be built into the development of the rider towards the next competition.

Child to adolescent to adult

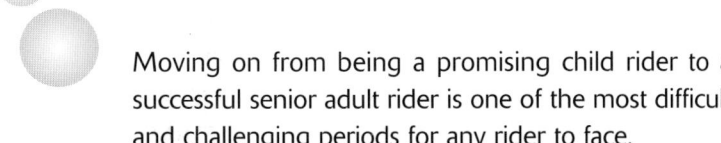

Moving on from being a promising child rider to a successful senior adult rider is one of the most difficult and challenging periods for any rider to face.

There are numerous issues which need to be addressed. We can itemise some of these changes and much consideration needs to be given to the specialist areas that these cover. The coach needs to be tactfully aware of all these aspects of development and able to balance them while focusing on the development of the riding skill.

Physiological changes
✦ Growth – height, weight – affecting balance and co-ordination.
✦ Hormonal/puberty.

Lifestyle changes
✦ School – college – university.
✦ Peer group influences.
✦ Boy/girl relationships.
✦ Social activities.
✦ Family/siblings.

Psychological changes
✦ Mental toughness.
✦ Self-belief.

All this, apart from the need for good horses!

SUMMARY

CHAPTER 8

▪ TEACHING CHILDREN IS CHALLENGING AND FUN; YOU ARE TAKING THE RESPONSIBILITY FOR THEIR INTRODUCTION TO EQUESTRIAN SPORT AND IT IS IN YOUR HANDS THAT THE EXPERIENCE IS A GOOD ONE AND LEADS TO A LIFELONG PASSION FOR THE SPORT.

▪ CONSIDER THE RIDERS' MENTAL AND PHYSICAL DEVELOPMENT AND ENSURE THEIR SAFETY AND WELFARE AT ALL TIMES.

▪ ENSURE THAT CHILDREN FEEL VALUED AND DEVELOP SELF-BELIEF WITHIN THEIR INDIVIDUAL LEVEL OF ABILITY.

▪ WITH TALENTED CHILDREN, INVOLVE THE PARENTS AND BE AWARE OF THE NEED TO SUPPORT THEM IN THEIR SPECIFIC ROLE.

▪ CONSIDER ALL THE ASPECTS IN THE DEVELOPMENT OF THE CHILD RIDER THROUGH ADOLESCENCE TO ADULTHOOD.

TOP TIPS TOP TIPS TOP TIPS TOP TIPS

- Enjoy teaching children: they are the future of the sport. As a coach, always learn from their spontaneity and innocence.

- Keep information clear and limited, let the child learn by 'finding out' and 'doing' then ask questions – the answers will sometimes surprise you!

- Keep sessions of concentrated 'learning' short and repeat the work in as many different ways as possible.

- Think of as many exercises as you can to keep things 'new' and different. Children keep you innovative.

- Enjoy finding a talented rider and, as you work with them, keep the parents informed and involved, and support them in the emotional journey they are also making.

WORKING WITH THE RECREATIONAL RIDER

THE TERMS 'PLEASURE' AND 'LEISURE' SEEM TO BE USED INTERCHANGEABLY THESE DAYS, BUT IF I AM RIGHT IN THINKING THAT PLEASURE MEANS *'A SOURCE OF GRATIFICATION/WHAT THE WILL PREFERS'*, WHILE LEISURE RELATES SIMPLY TO *'TIME FREE FROM EMPLOYMENT OR BUSINESS'*, THEN I CERTAINLY HOPE THAT EVERYONE'S PRIMARY REASON FOR RIDING AND BEING INVOLVED WITH HORSES IS FOR *PLEASURE.*

I am one of those few people in life who has managed to combine the pursuit I followed fanatically as a child in all my leisure time, which gave me so much pleasure, into a fulfilling and fruitful occupation as an instructor/coach. Few days go by when I do not count myself to be so fortunate to be able to earn a living through working with the animals that are my passion and aiming to transfer some of the expertise I have accrued over the years to people with the same passion that I have.

As an instructor/coach you will find, however, that the level of passion that *you* feel may not be the same with every pupil you are involved with. In the early stages of your work it is easy to apply your own perspective to the aims and ambitions of your riders, and this can seriously *inhibit* your ability to develop their riding and give them satisfaction. It is so important that, from an early stage of teaching different riders, you encourage them to tell you what *their* aims are for *this lesson, next week or next year.* You are probably saying at this moment, 'That's ridiculous, they don't know' and to a degree you are right, but it is up to you to guide them to know and to help them to discuss what is *realistic* as an expectation of a lesson. In this way they are far less likely to be disappointed and you will not have to work so hard to fulfil an expectation which is impossible to achieve.

In general, then, we should rarely be working with riders who 'do not want to be there' and are not interested in 'learning' to ride. In a wider context, unfortunately (for both them and their teachers), some children in school have no inclination whatsoever to be in class, let alone to take in any knowledge. It must be an uphill struggle for teachers to stimulate and motivate these poor youngsters to 'learn'. With riding, in most cases your pupils actually want to be there and improve.

Pleasure riders and the riding school

Let us consider the rider (adult or child) who takes up riding as their leisure pursuit and takes regular tuition in a riding school. Having learnt to ride myself in a riding school in my earliest years and then having run a riding school for nearly twenty years I can confidently state that there is no better environment in which to learn the basics of equestrianism. The only proviso to that statement is that it must be a GOOD riding school.

● *What will a rider taking lessons in a good riding school learn?*

● *Will a person learning to ride in a riding school be able to progress to competition and owning their own horse/pony?*

What can be learnt?

In a good riding school the rider will learn:

+ About personal safety around horses.
+ About basic safe clothing for being around and riding horses.
+ About basic saddlery and equipment for the horse.
+ About handling horses both in and out of the stable/field.
+ About leading, mounting and dismounting.
+ About riding on the lead rein/lunge rein/in small groups and individually.
+ About developing security and effectiveness in the position by working with and without stirrups in a safe environment.
+ About basic control and development of riding ability in walk, trot and canter.
+ About developing confidence in riding in closed and open order in an indoor and outdoor arena.
+ About developing the work through to the introduction of poles with a view to working over small jumps.
+ About having the confidence and independence to ride out in the fields and hack in small groups.
+ To take part in small 'in-house' competitions to develop skill and independence.
+ To understand basic care of the horse in a practical way and with some underpinning theoretical knowledge to give background to the practical competence.
+ To understand about the well-being of the horse in his working lifestyle.

Through sound and consistent instruction, a person learning to ride in a riding school develops a secure foundation of basic competence and horse management skills. This is enhanced by the rider usually riding a range of different horses, which develops versatility and effectiveness. Riding is a sport in which it takes *time* to establish as an *unconscious competence*. Ask any rider and they will tell you that YOU NEVER STOP LEARNING to ride.

• *Why is the previous statement so often heard with riding?*

The answer is simple – no two horses are the same and therefore every riding experience brings you something new to learn. The horse is a personality in his own right and much of the skill of riding at a higher level lies in developing and bringing out the horse's ability (in whatever sphere that might be) on the big occasion with that perfect partnership.

The weekly rider

If you are teaching the weekly pleasure rider you need to consider:

✦   Whether they are taking any other exercise during the week? (Do they walk the dog, swim, play sport at school, ride a bike – or do nothing else!)

✦   What is their 'normal' appearance, attitude. (Are they slim, muscularly toned, naturally athletic, overweight, clumsy in their management of their own body?)

✦   What their approach is to work in the lesson. (When you mention working without stirrups, do they complain?)

✦   Whether they are keen and self-motivated, asking questions and being enquiring about the progress of a session. ('Are we going to canter?' 'Can we jump?' Or 'I don't want to canter today'.)

Some 'peripheral' awareness of your rider's state of mind or activity during the week may also be helpful in enabling you to know how they are responding to your tuition. (For example, a rider who has had a gruelling day in the office and comes to ride to 'let go of some stress' doesn't need pressure in the lesson. On the other hand, a child rider on a Saturday morning with the whole exciting weekend ahead may be 'up for anything'!)

You will need to be more conscientious in your recap on the previous week's work with pupils who only ride for one hour a week. If a pupil is practising riding skills more than once a week then you can expect more retention of information and a quicker progression from *conscious incompetence* to *conscious competence*.

Group lessons and private tuition

There are certainly advantages and disadvantages to both of these.

Group lessons

Advantages

+ They are commercially much more viable than private lessons.
+ Riders (especially children) can learn from each other.
+ Riders gain confidence from each other.
+ Riders share experiences and have fun in a group.
+ It is easy to generate a competitive spirit to promote learning.
+ Horses/ponies may not need to work so hard.
+ Horses/ponies may work more happily in a group environment.

Disadvantages

+ Less opportunity to give individual help.
+ More challenging on the instructor to keep the situation safe, fun, active and controlled.
+ Can be challenging for less able riders to keep up, or for more capable riders to feel adequately stretched.
+ More outgoing personalities may dominate.
+ Less forthcoming personalities may feel sidelined.

Private lessons

Advantages

✦ Opportunity to provide individual help directed specifically at the rider's needs.

✦ Can support and nurture nervous riders or those lacking self-belief and confidence.

✦ Can develop the lesson at the rider's own rate of progress.

✦ In general, the instructor does not have to work so hard 'managing' a private lesson.

Disadvantages

✦ One-to-one sessions are labour-intensive and demanding on arena space.

✦ Can inhibit competitive development of riders because they are never required to measure themselves against other riders.

✦ Can give the rider a false impression of their own standard as they become 'protected' in their one-to-one situation.

Both private and group lessons have a place in a commercial riding school. However, the management should encourage group lessons at weekends and during busy times (e.g. school half-terms, etc.) as these enable more riders to be accommodated and, especially with children, develop riding ability more quickly.

It is of value that weekly riders learn to ride a variety of horses in order to develop their confidence and versatility. School horses tend to be adaptable and work according to the effectiveness of the rider. Many riding schools have horses who work sedately and with a docile attitude for beginner or novice riders and then 'raise their game' accordingly as the rider demonstrates more competence and effectiveness. A competent instructor can work with these horses to help them to increase their level of energy and the quality of their way of going by the exercises that they choose for the lesson (see Chapter 12).

Nervous riders

Nervousness in a rider is something that you will meet on a regular basis as an instructor/coach. Nervousness or anxiety is inhibiting, but on a horse it can be even more of a handicap as it may affect the horse's disposition.

Most beginner riders with little experience of horses 'know' the following facts as if they had had them indoctrinated into them since birth!

• Animals (horses) know when you are nervous and it makes them nervous. They can smell it!!

• When they put their ears back they are angry/unhappy/going to bite you.

• You aren't a rider until you have fallen off 3/7/? times. (This gives the novice rider a conviction that they are *going to fall off* because they can't ride!)

As we well know, these 'old wives' tales' are not without foundation, but unfortunately they can become a stronger factor in the novice rider's mind than is necessary and then the self-fulfilling prophecy situation may arise.

As an instructor/coach it will help considerably if you are aware of the confidence or nervousness of your riders so that you can 'manage' the situation to prevent the nerves creating a problem. In order to give maximum support and assistance to nervous riders, some fundamental questions have to be asked.

• *Why is the rider nervous?*

• *Have they always been nervous?*

• *Are they frightened of riding in general or is it one aspect of riding (e.g. canter or jumping) that they are fearful of?*

• *How do you recognise that the rider is nervous?*

The rider may be nervous because he or she:

• Is naturally a cautious person and tends to be anxious about an unknown situation until they have tried it and found they can do it.

• Has a perception (from a friend who has had a bad experience) that horses are dangerous creatures and that it is easy to fall off.

• Has had a bad experience (in a previous lesson) that has generated a natural fear of doing the activity again (e.g. lost balance and nearly fell off in canter).

• Is riding a horse who they know other riders have found difficult, even though they have never ridden him before.

• Has had a break from riding and is anxious that they may have lost some competence during their time out.

• Is tired, had a hard day at work/school and is feeling fragile generally and the riding just seems an effort too far.

• Has had an emotional crisis, fallen out with mother/ boyfriend/husband etc. and again is feeling fragile and not up to the challenge of taking control of a horse.

It is important that you learn to 'read' a pupil's mental state and confidence and plan your lesson accordingly. Subtle *questioning* may confirm your 'reading' and consolidate your decision for a certain lesson development. The lesson plan will then be structured to develop your rider's confidence and reassure them so that, at the end of the session, their anxiety level is considerably reduced. Encourage them to recognise the progression from very nervous to more at ease and also help them to recognise how they made that progressive step (or steps).

An example of how you might approach the issue would be:

• You recognise signs of anxiety (e.g. Fred says: 'I don't want to canter today', 'Can I not work without stirrups today', 'I don't like this horse, I nearly fell off him last time I rode him'.)

• In response to this you might say: 'We're not cantering or working without stirrups today, we are going to work on jumping position with our stirrups.'

- 'I know you are feeling a bit nervous Fred, but remember you have improved a lot since you last rode this horse and you *didn't* fall off even if it felt *nearly*.

- 'Now Fred, on a scale of 1 to 5, if 1 is very nervous and 5 is very relaxed, where is your anxiety level at the moment?' This will make Fred actually stop and *think* about his anxiety and assess it for himself. If he then says '1' you know he really is worried – he may even say minus something! If that happens you can make a small joke of it and say something to lighten the situation BUT register that he may really mean it. If he says 2 or 3 then you can say something on the lines of, 'Oh that's great – I really thought you were going to be on a 1 or minus 1'.

- Throughout the session you are then careful to monitor the work so that Fred has a good experience. Towards the end of the session, especially if Fred obviously begins to ride better, pick your moment to ask him again what his anxiety level is NOW?

- If he reassesses it as up one or two points then ask him what HE has done to move from the lower to the higher score. It is essential that he sees it as his achievement because then he takes ownership of the progression from nervous to less nervous. HE IS IN CONTROL.

- If he says the same as he started, then mildly chastise him for being negative and make him give an account of what he has done in the lesson and then be honest in his self-appraisal.

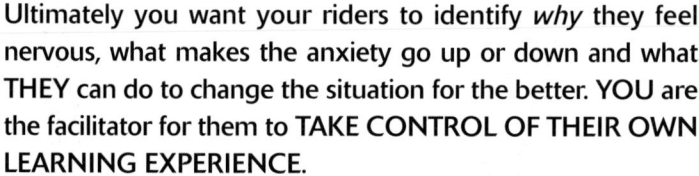

Ultimately you want your riders to identify *why* they feel nervous, what makes the anxiety go up or down and what THEY can do to change the situation for the better. YOU are the facilitator for them to TAKE CONTROL OF THEIR OWN LEARNING EXPERIENCE.

Riders who come to the sport later in life

There are many riders who come into this sport as a leisure pursuit in later life. There are various reasons for this. Perhaps they were never in a position as children to have the opportunity to ride (e.g. parents couldn't afford it, parents didn't support it). Alternatively, they may not have been interested in riding in their youth, but this interest was stimulated by an event later in their life (partner rides, they went to an equestrian competition and thought it looked great, saw someone learning to ride on TV, grandchildren started riding, etc.).

Taking up any sport later in life (not as a child or young adolescent) makes the 'learning' much more difficult (a point covered in the section on long term athlete development in Chapter 13). You, as an instructor/coach, must have due regard for

Older riders can bring many attributes to the sport.

the limitations of the rider coming into the sport later in life. However, motivation is the greatest stimulus so 'anything is possible' and such pupils will bring to their learning many attributes:

• If they have followed any other sport or practical skill they will have an orientation to 'learning' and often a strong commitment to 'work hard at it'.

• They will often have plenty of available assets to indulge their new passion, so will have many lessons and study the theory extremely diligently.

• They will have a greater concentration span than youngsters and will also often have very good reasoning powers about why and how to do things.

One of your responsibilities will be to regulate their learning to maximise the mature approach they bring to their lessons. They are likely to develop their theoretical knowledge much faster than their practical skills and this may be an inhibiter, as their enthusiasm for making progress is restricted by their own physical limitations. You need to maintain as much encouragement as you can. Try to arrange group lessons with riders in similar circumstances. You can also channel them into activities such as writing for a dressage judge, fence judging or helping in the administration of competitions; this will maintain their enthusiasm and allow them to see the technical difficulty of the sport they are following. Also, getting them involved in a Riding Club (some are now attached to some riding schools) will give more opportunity to mix socially and develop skills in horse care as well as the actual riding.

Riders returning to the sport

As mentioned in the previous chapter, riding is a sport that some parents build into the 'social skills list' for their developing offspring. Along with activities such as Brownies/Guides, Cubs/Scouts, Combined Cadet Force, football/rugby, swimming, dancing, etc. it is considered all part of a rounded upbringing. I must confess that

I subjected my own son (now grown up and definitely non-horsy) to learning to ride so that he was at least competent at the basics in case, at a later stage, he ever wants to go trekking in the foothills of the Himalayas or riding in New Zealand!

Many people who learn to ride as children may have a break of two or three decades but come back to it when time and finances allow. In my own career I have reintroduced many riders to the sport after they had taken a long break.

It is always useful to find out why a person is choosing to return to the sport:

✦ What has been their motivator?

✦ What are their expectations?

Some of the points we have already discussed in this chapter will be relevant again in this case. Often, the rider returning to the sport is quite humble about past standard or achievements and will often allow you to 'treat them as a beginner again'. I have had riders tell me 'That it is all so different from when I learnt to ride.' *Is that really true?* I don't think so. Surely, we are still looking for a harmonious partnership between horse and rider and the rider gaining enjoyment and pleasure from their riding.

Non-competitive riders

Many, many riders, both weekly riders and horse owners, *have no wish to* **compete**. Therefore, it is important that your perception is NOT that the ultimate experience of *every* rider is to be successful in competition. For many riders that is just not so. Countless people enjoy horses in a ways that do not involve them, personally, in competitive riding. This can range from occasional pleasure riding to training to high standards at home, and may include serious commitments of time and money such as breeding, having racehorses in training, or owning horses who are competed on their behalf by other riders who are more talented, have more time available or more motivation in that direction.

With such riders, your role again is to find out what their aims and aspirations are. (The fact that they don't wish to do Medium dressage or affiliated show jumping doesn't mean that they have none.) However, especially if they are newcomers to the sport and they truly do not know themselves, then you may have to guide them gently into making some choices and decisions. These must be right for them and in their best interests, to make them happy and content with their riding.

Contentment and partnerships between horse and rider are what pleasure riding is about and what is ultimately one person's pleasure might be very different for another. Your role may be to help a rider make choices appropriate to their circumstances, hopes and wishes.

SUMMARY

CHAPTER 9

■ AS PROFESSIONAL INSTRUCTORS/COACHES WE WILL OFTEN BE VERY INVOLVED WITH A LARGE PERCENTAGE OF LEISURE/PLEASURE RIDERS.

■ LEARNING TO RIDE IN A GOOD RIDING SCHOOL IMPARTS A WEALTH OF VALUABLE EQUESTRIAN SKILLS.

■ BE AWARE OF THE BALANCE, ADVANTAGES AND DISADVANTAGES BETWEEN PROVIDING PRIVATE OR GROUP SESSIONS FOR WEEKLY RIDERS.

■ BE ABLE TO 'READ' A RIDER'S CONFIDENCE LEVEL. USE QUESTIONS TO CONFIRM LEVEL OF CONFIDENCE AND EMPOWER THE RIDER TO TAKE CONTROL OF THEIR OWN ANXIETY LEVELS.

■ MANY RIDERS TAKE UP RIDING LATER IN LIFE OR RETURN TO THE SPORT AFTER A LENGTHY BREAK. RE-MOTIVATING THESE RIDERS CAN BE EXCITING AND CHALLENGING AND THEY MAKE A VALUABLE CONTRIBUTION TO MANY ASPECTS OF EQUESTRIANISM.

■ RESPECT THE IMPORTANCE AND VALUE OF THE NON-COMPETITIVE RIDER.

TOP TIPS TOP TIPS TOP TIPS TOP TIPS

■ Teaching in a good riding school for part of your career will equip you more fully as an instructor/coach than probably any other aspect of your personal development.

■ Learn to question carefully to assess a rider's confidence and motivation – it may not be the same as 'last week'.

■ Riders with past experience usually bring a steely commitment to improve; they have 'been there and done it' and have now made the conscious decision to come and try again – use that to your advantage to help them.

COACHING THE COMPETITION RIDER

AS WE DISCUSSED IN THE PREVIOUS CHAPTER, MANY RIDERS (IN FACT A LARGE PROPORTION OF PEOPLE WHO RIDE) ARE HAPPY TO ENJOY THEIR RIDING PURELY FOR THE PLEASURE IT GIVES THEM. FOR A FEW OTHERS THIS IS NEVER ENOUGH AND THE 'COMPETITIVE DRIVE' SHOWS FROM QUITE AN EARLY STAGE.

- *When does a 'pleasure' rider become a 'competition' rider?*
- *What drives a rider to want to compete?*

People, and what makes them 'tick', fascinate me. Questions I ask myself are:

- *What makes one person drive themselves to extremes to achieve and makes other people happy to 'sit on the sidelines' and observe'?*

- *What makes a child (of very young age) want to be 'the best in the world' or 'win a gold medal at the Olympics'?*

• *At what stage in their childhood did their talent and drive start to show and lead them to forge ahead of their peer group?*

• *Is it luck or chance that produces a top athlete – would they achieve even if their talent was not recognised and developed?*

At the time of writing, the record for a single-handed crossing of the Atlantic (3,000+ miles!) in a sailing boat is held by a young boy of just fourteen years of age.

Alan Sugar (boss of Amstrad and pioneer of the television series for 'go-getting' business entrepreneurs) is certainly a 'driven man', as is Richard Branson (head of the Virgin empire). In sport, consider people like Paula Radcliffe (athletics) and Wayne Rooney (football).

Recognising young talent

Relating back to Chapter 8 and the section on recognising exceptional talent in children, I would say that the early identification of ability and the subsequent nurturing of it will accelerate progress and the development of talent. Chapter 13 will give some information about systems and schemes, both national and international, which are directing sport towards the structured identification and development of talented athletes. Within these schemes, equestrian sport is identified as a 'late development' sport. This simply means that the skills of riding can be learnt and developed at a slightly later stage in a youngster's life than certain other sports, and this will not inhibit development or top achievement. (Sports such as gymnastics, swimming and tennis are all considered to be 'early development' sports. This means that the earlier the talent is identified, the easier it will be for the young athlete to establish the technical skills needed to maximise their potential.)

As a coach it is very exciting to discover talent. Even though riding is considered a 'late development' sport, in children, talent will usually show itself at a very early stage in their introduction to riding.

In a riding school children's class, and in Pony Club rallies, it is easy to recognise the child who has above average ability at a precocious age. The natural ability to 'sit well' on the pony, the ease with which the child appears to be able to carry out simple exercises – often coupled with a harmony with the pony that is not evident with any of the other riders in the group – singles out the individual as having exceptional ability.

Furthermore, the talented child will often show a passion to be involved with ponies/horses over and above 'just the riding'. Girls, especially, throw themselves into the whole aspect of grooming and caring for their pony/horse. Boys may show less interest in the 'caring', 'grooming', 'loving' part of pony/horse care, but it is important to realise that this does not necessarily mean that their talent or enthusiasm is less than that of the girls.

The eventing, dressage and show jumping organisations all run some kind of talent identification scheme. Riders with talent are then directed into a structure that will nurture that ability and develop it to maximum potential. It may be your good fortune as a coach to discover that one of your pupils is a potentially talented child and then it is important that you are able to give the support and direction necessary to assist the rider (and their parents) to maximise that talent.

From weekly rider to competitive rider

The 'weekly rider' may always have had a passion to compete and perhaps that has been one of their reasons for learning to ride in the first place. Other riders may gradually find that their weekly riding has developed into something that they want to do more of and they begin to look for bigger challenges.

● *How can you, the instructor/coach, meet this interest?*

✦   The riding school may run small competitions for 'in-house' pupils.

✦   The centre may be big enough to run 'outside' competitions, either affiliated or unaffiliated. In this case your pupil may become involved in the running of these shows (perhaps assisting in putting up jumps, stewarding or writing for the judge). This can often be the stimulus that then encourages the person to buy their first horse.

✦ Owning their first horse can then be the springboard that launches them into competing themselves.

✦ You might suggest that they join a local Riding Club and become involved initially helping with club activities. The next move, with their horse, will be to attend training clinics run by the club, and eventually perhaps they will be keen to ride for a club team.

✦ Youngsters can foster the competitive 'bug' by attending competitions to watch their idols. If really fortunate, they may be taken under the wing of a competitive rider and allowed to watch and learn 'on the job'. In accompanying said rider they will learn in a 'hands-on' environment, then develop into a valuable member of the support team.

Motivation

• What is motivation?

• What affects motivation?

• Why are some people so much more motivated than others?

• Is it emotion that excites a sportsperson (or artist, mountaineer, sailor, etc.) to action?

• Is it always necessary to be self-motivated or can someone motivate you to maximum effect or success?

• What motivates YOU (as a coach; as a rider – and are the motivations the same?)

We might answer the first question by saying that:

✦ Motivation is incentive.

✦ Motivation is personal drive.

It is also, in my opinion:

+ Certainly a 'state of mind' that is variable in many athletes.
+ A potentially fragile state that is very vulnerable in certain conditions, but these conditions vary from one person to another.
+ Not consistently guaranteed with competition riders, however successful they are.

Regarding self-motivation and the motivation of the coach, I would say that motivating the rider is a *responsibility* of the coach, BUT it is never the *sole responsibility* of the coach. It must be jointly nurtured by *communication* between coach and pupil.

Factors that can affect motivation

Factors that can affect motivation positively include:

+ Successful achievement motivates people to work for more success.
+ Peer pressure (including peer success).
+ Praise and encouragement from a competitor's coach, loved ones, younger or less able competitors (seeing the competitor as a role model).
+ Public accolade.
+ Own sense of well-being and excitement.

Factors that can affect motivation negatively include:

+ Fear of failure.
+ Lack of self-belief.
+ Fatigue, lack of fitness for the mental and physical demands of the sport.
+ Pressure from coach or other competitors.
+ High expectations from those around the competitor based on past achievements.
+ Loss of form.

✦ Over-training.

✦ Seasons and weather conditions.

✦ Loss of confidence in relationship with coach.

Factors crucial to fostering motivation

Two factors mentioned in earlier chapters are crucial to fostering and protecting motivation. COMMUNICATION becomes the essential tool in maintaining the morale of your competitive pupil and AWARENESS is a fundamental requisite for the coach. Especially with children and adolescents, the state of motivation can be very fragile and fluctuate from one week to another or one competition to another. It may be your role at times to act as a confidante for your pupils, so that they trust you and are able to share their concerns and worries with you. In this way you are most able to help them through a potential time of de-motivation and decide how best to assist them in re-establishing their self-drive and incentive to succeed.

The coach's drive

Your own drive and motivation may at times far outstrip that of your pupil. Be aware that this is potentially dangerous ground for a coach to be on for a prolonged period.

● *Why is this situation likely to occur?*

✦ Particularly if you are coaching a child or adolescent rider, your own knowledge of the sport will be more refined and superior to that of your pupil.

✦ A young rider (and their parents) may be totally unaware of their potential ability and thus unable to understand the effort and commitment that may be required to develop the talent that you have identified.

As the coach, it is important that you develop the rider's awareness of:

(a) Their potential talent.
(b) The long pathway that they may need to follow to realise their ability.

YOU MUST NOT take sole responsibility for structuring the rider and planning the entire route with appropriate goals and start to 'drive' the whole development. If you do, the rider (and supporters) will allow you to take on the entire responsibility for the rider's progress and when the achievement falters the fault will lie with YOU – the coach. Instead, your roles are to:

✦   Develop the pupil's self-motivation, to help them recognise goals and plan the training towards achieving them. (*Planning*, discussed in detail in Chapter 6, is a key factor in success at all times, but it is especially important for the competitive rider. Essential for the rider who wants to do well in their club's Novice dressage test, it becomes ever more important at the higher levels, when timescales may be measured in months or even years, and attention to detail on many fronts must be phenomenal.)
✦   Monitor your pupil's motivation, and support and nurture it when it is affected by some of the circumstances mentioned previously.

The rider's motivation

Ultimately, an athlete's progress will be SELF-DRIVEN. It can be supported, nurtured, enhanced, encouraged by coach, parents, siblings, friends, peer pressure and perhaps other coaches, but progress will only reach its FULL POTENTIAL if the rider wholeheartedly embraces his or her own motivation.

In my own experience I have seen really talented riders achieve to a less high standard than their potential because 'their heart was not really in it', even though they were very well supported by all around them. Conversely, I have seen less innately talented riders achieve beyond everyone's expectations because they took every opportunity to drive themselves to the maximum and took full responsibility for their own progress.

You will know the rider who just 'expects to win' on the day and they don't win. The follow-up goes something like this:

- *'I was just about to do my test and the judge took a break so when I went in it was ten minutes later than my time and the horse had gone off the boil.'*
(The horse doesn't know what time he is due to compete; the rider makes the excuse that the horse had been worked in for too long.)

- *The test was going really well and then someone spooked him by walking past the arena with an umbrella.'*
(The horse must be sufficiently 'on the aids' and 'through' that he doesn't spook at anything but, if he does, the rider is so focused that the partnership is reassured and harmony re-established within a minimal time.)

- *'I've always beaten the other riders at other competitions so I know it's just because the judge doesn't like me.'*
(Judges actually judge what is happening in front of them on the day – they do not have personal likes and dislikes of riders!)

- *'He was clear and then the silly horse hit the last fence and had it down.'*
(Perhaps the rider thought they had jumped a clear round and lost concentration, so allowing the horse to lose balance and pay for it with the last fence down.)

Dealing with success and failure

Expectations

Before considering success and failure we need to explore EXPECTATIONS, since these precede the activity which produces success or failure and, indeed, help to define them. If a rider is *expectant* of something, they are anticipating (for better or worse) that it is likely to happen. If, for example, a rider 'expects' that their horse may have difficulty with a particular dressage movement or fence, but the horse copes with it well, then the rider is likely to view the outing as a relative success, even if they don't achieve a particularly high placing. However, if positive expectations are not fulfilled (e.g. the rider expects to 'nail' the simple changes, but fluffs them) then they can become despondent and de-motivated as the realisation that what they expected to happen didn't do so. Expectations must therefore be realistic and linked to achievable goals.

Someone who starts riding at the local riding school once a week and has expectations of being able to compete at Badminton Horse Trials in a year's time is going to be disappointed. It is your role as the coach of such a person to realign their expectations to a goal that is achievable and therefore exciting to work towards, because the end goal is visible and achievable. The other side of the coin is that it is so easy to make excuses for not coming up to (achievable) expectations. The top competitors NEVER make excuses for anything; they apply what they've learnt from an unwanted turn of events to controlling the next circumstances in which such a pattern may repeat itself so that it doesn't.

Success

It is easy to deal with success because it is ENJOYABLE!

Success builds confidence.

Confidence develops further competence and success.

Success develops self-belief.

It is very important that, as the coach, you allow your pupils to enjoy their success and, in fact, that you build it into your development plan. It should become an important part of your pupils' *motivation*.

Success is enjoyable!

If your *planning* and *goal-setting* (see Chapter 6) have been well structured, then achievement and success *should* develop naturally from these. The rider should then feel confident and secure in their success and not feel that it was a 'one off' and more 'by luck than judgement'.

The rider must increasingly feel *in control of their success* and, without becoming complacent, be confident that, with the appropriate training, warming up of horse and self, then delivery of the work expected in competition, they will achieve a successful result.

If, on the other hand, the rider feels that a win was a 'one off' or 'lucky chance', and that they were not in control of the success, then the 'chance' of repeating that success is unlikely. They may then go into the next competition worrying that they may not do as well and this becomes a self-fulfilling prophecy.

In summary, the rider must feel that success is achieved through a systematic plan of preparation, work and delivery that assures the positive outcome.

While allowing the rider to enjoy a period of 'glory' in their success and, in fact, encouraging this because this becomes a future *motivator*, the coach must then encourage the rider to move on, as there will always be those coming from behind wishing to move up into the 'top spot' to win.

The success is then built into the further *planning* of the future work.

Failure

Failure can be defined as 'lack of success', 'falling short of achieving a level of competence', but there is also the concept that, if you fail 'someone' then you disappoint them. In failing to achieve (often in competition) a rider may feel that they have failed themselves and that they have failed those around them (parents, supporters and coach). The way in which you, as coach (and others around them) deal with a rider's failure can either help them address the disappointment, or cause the lack of success to affect them adversely for the future, both in the short and long term.

Assessing the reasons for failure

Failure may be a result of:

✦   Lack of *preparation*.

✦   Loss of concentration.

✦   Careless or casual approach.

✦   Lack of self-discipline on the rider's part. (Partying the night before and a late night caused rider to be tired/not feeling 100%.)

✦   Horse not quite fit enough/not concentrating (spooked at disturbance).

✦   Rider put off by competition environment. (Course too big, too difficult, opposition too 'hot.') All these are circumstances that affected the rider's mental state before starting (negative feelings).

✦   Some 'bad luck' beyond rider's control. (Unavoidably held up on journey to competition so arrived late and warm-up limited. First to go in the class – rider considers this an 'unlucky' draw.)

Addressing the reasons for failure

● The first and most important criterion for addressing failure is that the rider must agree the reason for failure and, if the reason was the rider's inadequacy, then the rider must *take responsibility* for change.

● Without the rider accepting this responsibility, any changes you as coach make may be unabsorbed and vulnerable, unless the rider wholeheartedly takes on the commitment to the improvement.

● Therefore discussion between rider and coach is essential, with a thorough 'debrief' of the performance. The debrief must be both from the rider's and coach's viewpoints and there are likely to be differences.

● Remember, however, that the rider is 'living and carrying out' the performance and you are only observing it. You have the huge advantage of *all your concentration* being on the horse and rider in front of you, whereas your rider has to make instant judgements about what to do. It is so easy to think 'What on earth made her do that?' when you (with time and experience on your side) would have done something else!

• Allow the rider to explain what they did and, more importantly, why they chose to do it – *really listen to the reasons and think about the answer as the rider felt it* – before you become judgemental and start voicing a different opinion. The rider does not need to feel immediately that he or she was 'wrong' and you are unhappy.

• The *timing* of a debriefing on failure can also be essential to rebuilding shattered confidence or in turning the poor performance around into a motivating and positive driver to be better 'next time'.

I have seen many occasions immediately after a poor jumping round or dressage test a rider being approached by parents, supporters and sometimes by a less experienced coach. The rider has barely drawn breath and is immediately asked to give an opinion of their performance. If they have had the last fence down, they focus strongly on the 'not a clear round'. If they have missed a simple change or the horse moved in the halt, again they focus on the mistakes. They can often be abrasive and even aggressive as the adrenalin is still running and their immediate emotion is one of disappointment and not doing as well as they had hoped.

Therefore, as a coach, learn to *observe first* and *plan* the timing of the debriefing. Often, the parents or nearest supporters can never say the right thing! If they say, 'Well done, that looked great!' the rider will explode, giving every reason as to why it was an appalling performance. If they commiserate, believing that there were some problems, the rider is just as likely to tear into them for thinking it was not good when in fact the rider thought it was fine! This, I can assure you, is the result of the rider's tension venting its escape route through the person nearest or first into conversation. (I always feel incredibly sorry for top competitors who have to learn to deal with television reporters who thrust microphones under their nose immediately as they finish a major sporting performance. Whether the outcome is good – easier to radiate goodwill – or bad, they have to maintain composure and give some relevant comments on their performance at a time when they maybe just want to be completely on their own to reflect and 'cool down' mentally and physically.)

In your coaching it can be helpful to consider the following points when discussing a competitive performance with a rider:

• The better you know your pupil, the more you will know how much they want to talk and how soon after a performance.

• In any case, you need to encourage them (in your regular training sessions) to recognise the importance of *reflection* on a past performance and discussion or debrief of this in detail.

• Allow the rider to lead the conversation. When they ask questions like: 'What did you think?' 'How did it look?' 'Wasn't he fabulous?' learn to 'read' the question or statement and, if in doubt, agree or keep the reply very non-confrontational. For example, the easiest response to, 'What did you think?' is 'How did it ride?' This way, you put the ball back in the rider's court to let you know how *they* were feeling about the ride. 'How did it look?' could be given the response: 'How did it feel?' You let the rider tell you and then you can agree in a general way. Now is not the time to start an in-depth consideration of the strengths and weaknesses of a round.

• I often encourage a rider to have a proper cool down, put the horse away (with help) and then, sitting down with a drink, encourage the rider to tell you how it went.

• Further to the previous point, it is valuable to educate parents or other supporters as to the importance of the moments *immediately* after the rider has completed the competition, and of being available to assist (e.g. rug on horse, coat for rider, drink for rider, help with cooling horse, etc.).

• If your pupils get into this type of routine they will become confident to *reflect* and be self-critical and constructive about what they need to improve on and what was good.

• It can also be useful to encourage your riders to keep a diary of their competition programme. This will help them to be aware of their feelings and emotions prior to and during a competition and how these affected the performance.

Success and failure are not unique to competition riders – *all* riders will experience the feelings of success and failure on many occasions during their riding endeavours. These feelings are perfectly appropriate but you, as the coach, must be aware of the part they can play in affecting the rider's confidence, motivation and self-belief, as well as overall enjoyment.

Any sport has huge variations in periods of success and failure, highs and lows for participants. This is one of the most 'character-building' aspects of participating in sport. With equestrian sport there is the added consideration of the horse. When the rider is focused, motivated, trained and prepared for competition the horse may be lame. When the horse is firing on all cylinders the rider may be injured or not on form. Every aspect of planning and preparation can be covered and then a brief moment of 'bad luck' or an unpredictable circumstance can rob the partnership of 'certain' success. (Can anyone not sympathise with the dilemma that caused Bettina Hoy to lose an Olympic Gold medal – both team and individual – in Athens in 2004?)

The coach therefore has an ongoing 'balancing act' in keeping the competitive rider motivated, planning their programme, helping them be realistic about their aims and dealing with the success and failure that any competition throws at us all. Remember that the *responsibility* is a joint one – it is not a matter only for you, the coach. If you take on the full responsibility, then you will also have to carry the disappointments completely for the rider as they will unconsciously put the 'blame' or responsibility *on you*. Therefore, plan everything jointly, with the rider taking much of the initiative and you guiding them to make the decisions that are in their best interests. The responsibility is then more with them and they will then accept the same responsibility if the outcome is not as successful as aimed for.

SUMMARY

CHAPTER 10

■ SOME RIDERS (USUALLY FROM QUITE EARLY ON) BECOME COMPETITIVELY ORIENTATED AND THIS PROVIDES 'SELF-MOTIVATION'.

■ IN YOUR PROFESSIONAL CAPACITY AS A COACH, RECOGNISE TALENT AND ENTHUSIASTICALLY HELP DIRECT AND PRODUCE IT.

■ MOTIVATION CAN BE A POTENTIALLY FRAGILE AND VERY VARIABLE STATE FOR THE RIDER.

■ EXPECTATIONS MUST BE REALISTIC AND LINKED TO ACHIEVABLE GOALS.

■ SUCCESS AND FAILURE ARE INTRINSIC PARTS OF DEALING WITH COMPETITION.

TOP TIPS TOP TIPS TOP TIPS TOP TIPS

TOP TIPS

■ Be a positive and realistic coach.

■ Allow your competition rider to 'lead'; support them and agree goals for their progress.

■ Learn to know your competition riders. 'Read' them and know how and when to motivate them.

■ Be supportive in a rider's failure but don't take on all the responsibility for lack of achievement.

A CAREER IN EQUESTRIAN COACHING

IF YOU WERE TO ASK MOST CHILDREN IN THE EARLY STAGES OF THEIR INVOLVEMENT WITH HORSES WHAT THEIR LONG-TERM AIM WAS, THE MAJORITY WOULD PROBABLY HAVE LITTLE OR NO IDEA. I WOULD SUSPECT THAT VERY FEW YOUNG RIDERS LEARNING TO RIDE WOULD SEE THEMSELVES AS FUTURE INSTRUCTORS, JUST AS MOST CHILDREN LEARNING GEOGRAPHY OR MATHS IN SCHOOL WOULD PROBABLY NOT TELL YOU THAT THEIR AIM IN LIFE WAS TO TEACH THE SAME.

So, what is the trigger that leads someone to think about becoming a riding coach? And how does their career evolve? In truth, the answers are likely to vary from person to person, but if I give a brief rundown of my own career, it may be that some of my early circumstances strike chords with certain readers, and/or provide food for thought – although I am not suggesting that everyone should enter the profession exactly as I did.

Referring back to my introduction to this book, it was always my aim to ride and to be involved with horses for my entire life, and I recognised at a very early stage that my pathway to this goal lay in teaching people to ride.

I came from a middle-class background with totally non-horsy parents, who were not prepared to expend all their time and money just to allow their second daughter to indulge her passion for horses. While I desperately wanted to ride and compete it was just not possible for me to do so. However, my personal drive and determination to achieve caused me to work every hour that I could snatch at a local dealing yard/riding school, where I learnt to 'sit on anything' because the longer I stayed on some lunatic, the more I got given to ride. (Usually another lunatic that no one else would take on!)

I was prepared to ride anything with four legs and from that position I worked my way into being able to compete on horses who were to be sold, and I started jumping in Junior and then Young Rider classes. When I reached the age of 16 my parents decided that I could have a horse for two years before going to university, so I had the first horse who was truly my own. From that point on, vowed to myself that I would never be without a horse of my own again.

I quickly realised that if I went to university and 'got a proper job' I would have to relinquish the path I was beginning to tread towards a profession in the equestrian industry. I had also begun to get some satisfaction from helping other aspiring youngsters at the riding school to enjoy their ponies/horses and learn to ride. I realised that, to make a career in the horse industry, I would need to 'teach' as this would be the source of income by which I could ride and compete. For me the pathway was clear – I did not say easy! When I started in the early 1970s the only professional qualifications were the British Horse Society Assistant Instructor's Certificate, (BHSAI), the British Horse Society Instructor (BHSI) and then the Fellowship of the British Horse Society (FBHS). Without elaborating further on my personal history this was the road I took and, through earning a living as a professional instructor/coach, I have been able to develop my own riding and competitive experience first through show jumping, then some eventing and in more recent years with more specialisation in dressage.

During my career I have been fortunate enough to train with many fantastic teachers of equestrian sport; some are sadly no longer with us, and others are forging a hugely successful path both nationally and internationally. As my own position in the sport has developed I have been privileged indeed to mix with and learn from some of the greatest figures in equestrian sport, including Goran 'Yogi' Breisner (eventing) and Jennie Loriston-Clarke (dressage) to name just two.

Basic requisites for coaching

It is my experience that great trainers and coaches come from various different backgrounds, but there are some essentials they have in common:

• There *must* be an underlying love of the horse and the patience and commitment to look after the interests of the horse *first and foremost.*

• I cannot think of anyone I have come across as a coach of equestrian sport who has never sat on a horse.

There is a statement often made about teachers and coaches (in all sports) that I think is rather unkind and often very unjustified: 'Those who *can*, compete and those who *can't*, teach.' Let's explore this opinion a little more thoroughly.

To ride competitively and to a high level in any discipline of equestrian sport requires a substantial source of revenue. Riding is often seen as an 'elitist sport', the domain of the rich. This is *not* true but just like sailing and motor racing it requires 'equipment and facilities' that are very costly. (If your offspring aspire to wield a tennis racquet or snooker cue it is very likely that their talent in this sport will be much easier to develop without the need for such a deep pocket.) Thus there are riders who have not been able to compete at a high level because of lack of horse power, who nonetheless are talented and knowledgeable and develop the skills to become valuable coaches. On the other hand, there are talented and successful competition riders who lack the empathy or communication skills to be top coaches. Coaching successfully requires passion, excellent communication skills, a good eye and experience of the sport.

• *Should a coach ALWAYS have been a competitor too and, if so, to what level?*

This debate will run and run and there will be different opinions that all have some validity to the extent that I don't believe there is a 'right' or 'wrong' answer. I do believe however that:

• A rider can be a successful competitor BUT (as just explained) is not therefore automatically a good instructor or coach.

• A coach can be good without having necessarily ridden at a high level, however, it is certainly an *advantage* if the coach has ridden at a higher level than their pupils.

• If a coach is someone who develops an existing skill, that skill must first have been *well taught* (not necessarily by the coach).

• Some teachers can also coach, and many coaches are excellent teachers. However, where distinctions exist between coaching and teaching, it may be the case that some individuals are better at one aspect than the other.

Watching coaching in any sport is fascinating and I can always learn from seeing other coaches practise their profession.

In addition to the fundamental qualities mentioned earlier, I believe that good coaches have several other criteria in common:

✦ They are patient.
✦ They can communicate.
✦ They have sympathy and empathy with their pupils.
✦ They listen to their pupils.
✦ They can motivate, encourage and inspire.

Developing and specialising

Equestrian sport has expanded in popularity over the last three decades and nowadays we in Britain probably have a competition structure in all disciplines as highly developed as any country worldwide. Expansion in competition generates more interest in learning to ride and this in turn generates a requirement for more instructors and coaches for both learners and competitors.

When I started my career as a 'riding instructor', I (and many of my contemporaries starting up the career ladder through the British Horse Society qualifications) taught many beginner and novice riders, many Pony Club rallies and some Riding Club clinics. As a result of this I taught much 'general horsemanship', i.e. basic riding on the flat and basic pole work and jumping. It is still the case that many young instructors coming into equestrian teaching would expect to 'cut their teeth' in general teaching. From this you learn the basic skills of:

✦ Managing a class.
✦ Learning to recognise nervous riders, awkward riders, those not trying or lacking concentration.
✦ Planning and developing lessons (both class and private).
✦ Managing parents, siblings, awkward ponies/horses, etc.

All this experience prepares the young instructor/coach for being able to move on into a specialist area if this is their ultimate choice.

Many coaches will only have an interest in one discipline, perhaps dressage or show jumping. The coaches who see themselves as 'event' specialists will, by the nature of the discipline of 'eventing', need to be all-round in their teaching skill, as the eventer may need help in dressage, show jumping or cross-country training.

Again, it is very easy to enter into some strong debate as to the merits of someone 'being able to teach jumping' when 'I only teach dressage riders'. I believe that if we teach better horsemanship then we will develop better riders who, in turn, will have a wider regard for the horse's well-being. I also believe strongly that a 'dressage rider' is a much more established, deeper, more feeling rider if they have jumped (any horse). They will have a greater awareness of their own balance and that of the horse and they will often be a braver rider than the rider who 'never jumps'. Further to this, often a horse will benefit greatly by the rider 'getting off his back' and giving him a good canter in a forward seat. Other horses veritably thrive on doing some pole work or jumping it cheers them up, makes them think forward and keeps them happier.

Show jumping specialists will also broaden their skill and expertise if they recognise the huge part flatwork plays in the training of the show jumping; horse and rider. Watch any top show jumping coach and see how much time they spend on the horse's balance, in canter especially, and the rider's balance in relation to the horse.

To summarise, young coaches will severely limit their options for developing their skills as professional coaches if they specialise too early. It is far better to first develop an all-round competence, as this will make you a more versatile and flexible coach. As you develop, you may wish to specialise in the area of your own competition expertise or in the area that interests you most, but your broad experience will enable you to help clients in any aspect of their development.

A foot in every camp

The British Horse Society's professional qualifications up to BHSI level deliberately cover all aspects of good riding and horsemastership and teaching. A BHSI (International level 3) is therefore capable of running an equestrian business and being in charge of the teaching of dressage and jumping up to a good competitive standard (Advanced Medium dressage, Intermediate eventing and Foxhunter level show jumping).

Of course, any qualification only conveys recognition of your competence to a level on the day of examination. It should mean:

• That you worked hard to identify the competences required of you by the relevant examination syllabus.

• That you then worked on a plan of personal development to ensure that you could fulfil the requirements.

• That your preparation then enabled you to deliver the demonstration of your competence on the exam day.

• That you were able to deal with the increased pressure that an examination environment may put on you and still delivered the standard required (very like a competition).

BUT no qualification is worth the paper it is written on unless you are committed to your own CONTINUOUS PERSONAL DEVELOPMENT. There is one sure thing in this world and that is that *nothing stays the same*; there is always *change and evolution*. It is impossible to 'stand still'; it is only possible to move forward and improve, or by not moving forward to stagnate and risk deteriorating.

The more you care about your profession and your own competence as a coach the more you will strive to:

✦ Learn from every situation or opportunity.

✦ Reflect on what you do or have done; what worked and what needs adjusting or changing.

✦ Review and introduce new options to your work.

✦ Consider on a regular basis how you can improve your own coaching.

✦   Ask other's opinions on coaching subjects, question your own practice and thinking.

✦   Consider asking a more experienced coach (or mentor) to observe you in action and give constructive *feedback* on how you can improve.

Feedback

- *What is feedback?*
- *When should we ask for feedback?*
- *When should we use feedback?*

Observation and analysis lead to evaluation, which should start and finish with the rider and generate feedback.

Feedback is a two-way process. In order to develop skill riders need feedback.

Feedback should be:

- Appropriate.
- Accurate.
- Constructive.
- Delivered with thought and relevant 'timing'.

Criticism:

- Should be used sparingly.
- May evoke a defensive or negative reaction.
- Focuses on the problem rather than the solution.
- May be difficult to accept.

Praise:

- Improves confidence.
- Is the opposite of criticism.
- Should be sincere.
- Should be appropriate.
- Should be deserved.

Advice:

- Should be developed in most appropriate ways.
- May be open-ended.
- May be directive and assume a 'right' way of doing things.
- Is particular to each individual coach (relates to own values and beliefs).

Guided self-discovery:

- Is less directive and evaluative than other options.
- Requires the coach to use questioning and listening skills.

Feedback is another of those valuable coaching tools. Feedback is usually a response that we have asked for (possibly from a pupil or another coach) that gives us *information*. This information can be a guideline for future development. With this input (feedback) we are then able to improve quality or make corrections.

Feedback is the product of *questioning and listening*. It is vital to the development of training. Ask for feedback regularly and often. It can give you the key to assessment and evaluation and help greatly in the future *planning* of a lesson or programme of work (several lessons).

In the context of the professional coach, feedback can also help us greatly in our own quest for personal development and improvement. One of the most revealing experiences I have had in recent years as a coach was when I was training about thirty other coaches in a personal development session. I asked them to write down one attribute that they liked about me (I was the visiting coach from overseas) and one thing they didn't like! I asked them to do the same for their own regular chief instructor who was also their boss! After dismissing the group, the two of us looked at the comments that were on yellow sticky 'post-it' notes around the room. The comments about me ranged from 'she comes to help us' to 'smiley' and 'firm'. The comments about my colleague ranged from 'moody', 'bad tempered' to 'makes us work' (remember, the instructors knew this person very well as their boss!). My colleague was appalled that the comments were fairly damning and I had to offer encouragement that the opinion formed about someone you know well is often different from the opinion that you have on initial meeting, or when you only know a person superficially.

Nevertheless, this emphasised to me the need to consider how others see you: it is often not how you see yourself and you must try to understand why someone sees you as they do. It may be as simple as you being an adult and they, as a child, see you as a person in authority and scary. Alternatively, if you are a coach who has been a successful competition rider and have an image and 'important person status' about you, a rider may feel very inhibited by you and not be brave enough to tell you their worries and inadequacies in case you think they are 'useless'.

Always be approachable and remember to try to find out how a person sees you or feels about you – it may help you be able to communicate with them and therefore help the development of your training.

✦ Are you open to other people's perceptions of you?

✦ Are you open to feedback?

As a coach you must be open to feedback; you will then 'grow' and your personal development will not be limited.

Employment

Many things are automated these days and many practical manual occupations are very mechanised, but horses will never be looked after by computers or be able to fit into a neat 38-hour week! Working in the equestrian industry is hard and challenging and no one should be doing it if they don't have a true vocational love for it. It will never make you a member of the 'idle rich'!

That said, committed, hard-working horse lovers are really worth their weight in gold and can and should command respect and get a good living in the industry. If they have taken the trouble to learn their skills well and have some kind of qualification to add weight to their practical hands-on competence, employment should be guaranteed.

These days it is very easy to ensure that employment offers what it has promised. An interview should reveal the expectations of employer and employee. The potential employee should go to the interview armed with a written list of questions about the position, which should be answered clearly.

For a young instructor/coach it is reassuring and motivating to be in your first teaching position in a place where there is a more senior coach above you. This will give you the confidence to 'learn the trade' with someone to turn to and others to watch for your own personal development. For young instructors holding the British Horse Society Preliminary Teaching Test, who are aiming to gain teaching experience prior to holding the BHSAI certificate, a position in a British Horse Society approved establishment ensures that the teaching will take place in a safe and regulated environment.

A wage or salary is assured and not dependent on 'having a good week' of private clients. Full-time employment will also convey benefits such as PAYE and National Insurance contributions; there may also be such perks as a private health insurance scheme and some kind of regulated pension incentive.

Continuous personal development may be encouraged through the establishment that employs you and training may be part of the package. It may also be possible to keep a horse and have an opportunity to compete, and this can assist if you are striving to further your competitive record as well as fulfilling a need to earn a living.

If you are employed by a big commercial establishment or an equestrian college, then competitions, training seminars and lecture demonstrations may be run at the venue – and also, possibly, BHS exams. All these options can enhance your knowledge and experience of running commercial activities, as well as helping you to further your own level of training and expertise.

Self-employment

After working for a variety of employers you may decide it is time to 'go it alone'. You may choose to set up your own training establishment, riding school or livery yard. This can be hugely satisfying and very rewarding but it is a big commitment and can be very lonely when everything is not running smoothly.

Some of the pros and cons might motivate you towards or against taking the plunge and setting up your own business.

For:

• You are 'your own boss'. You call the shots *but* the 'buck also stops with you'.

• You can work as hard as you like and you know it is all 'for you'.

- You can direct the business exactly as you wish.

- If you have a good business brain and are innovative then you may be able to develop a good living. There are plenty of people who want to learn to ride and be actively involved with buying and keeping horses, buying horse equipment, etc.

- If you learn to delegate well and manage your staff well, then you can be in charge of a happy workforce and they will repay you with loyalty and reliability.

- When things are going well it is great to be in charge!

- If you are a self-motivated individual then this might be the way for you to go.

Against:

- When things are difficult, if you are a sole boss it is lonely and hard work.

- When staff let you down or are difficult to recruit or retain then the horses still need looking after – by you!

- Your livery owners, clients, etc. will still expect a full service from you even when you are feeling under the weather, have flu, want to leave the yard early, or have a weekend off!

- It is very difficult to be 'off duty' especially if you live on site and your clients have your home and mobile phone numbers.

- The business is a major tie and responsibility 7 days a week, 365 days a year.

- It is easy to never find time for yourself and become engulfed by your commitment to the business.

Freelancing

Some people might think that self-employment and freelancing are synonymous. Whereas I used the former term to refer to running a business with a permanent base and other employees, I'm using 'freelancing' to refer to a more 'nomadic' existence, teaching at other people's premises and employing no one else. I ran an equestrian business of the former type in a partnership for nearly 20 years and without doubt they were some of the happiest days of my life and it was hugely satisfying having a base from which to work. The business enabled me to have facilities where I could teach and train my own and other people's horses as well as many career students. It was a period when our business could support running a lorry and several competition horses and enable us as proprietors to compete on a regular basis. My dream of working full time with horses *and* having the resources to indulge my own competitive development was fulfilled. However, freelancing in the last decade or so has been just as satisfying and has opened up more and more opportunities. The pros and cons of freelancing can also be clearly identified:

For:

• If you have developed a name for yourself and a sound reputation as a coach you will be much sought-after as a freelance coach.

• There can be lots of variety.

• You can choose when you work and how often.

• You are not tied by a business or horses that have to be looked after day in, day out.

• You can plan your own diary and take time off to do whatever you want. (Badminton, Horse of the Year Show, Olympia, you name it!)

Against:

• The work may be seasonal; there may be quiet periods.

• You may have to learn to say 'no' to things.

• You will need to be prepared to travel.

• You may not always be working in ideal circumstances.

• You will not have a base to work from and it can be difficult to keep a competition horse 'up and running'.

• If you are earning enough to run a lorry, some horses and fund your competing, then you don't have enough time to ride and if you have enough time to ride then you may not be earning enough to fund the habit!

SUMMARY

CHAPTER 11

■ A CAREER IN THE EQUESTRIAN INDUSTRY IS HUGELY SATISFYING AND REWARDING BUT MUST COME FROM 'THE HEART'.

■ MOST COACHES WILL HAVE HAD SOME COMPETITIVE EXPERIENCE – THE LEVEL IS NOT NECESSARILY THAT IMPORTANT.

■ A VERSATILE COACH WHO HAS SKILL IN DRESSAGE AND JUMPING TRAINING WILL BE ABLE TO SPECIALISE LATER AND WILL ALWAYS FIND A VALUED NICHE.

■ FEEDBACK IS A VALUABLE TOOL IN COACHING BUT IS ALSO HELPFUL BETWEEN COACHES TO IMPROVE PERSONAL DEVELOPMENT.

■ FULL-TIME EMPLOYMENT GENERALLY GIVES SECURITY FOR A LESS EXPERIENCED COACH.

■ SELF-EMPLOYMENT CAN ALLOW THE COACH TO DEVELOP IN THEIR OWN PARTICULAR AREA OF STRENGTH OR INTEREST.

■ FREELANCING CAN ALLOW SCOPE AS A COACH WITHOUT THE TIES OF HAVING A BUSINESS TO RUN.

TOP TIPS   TOP TIPS   TOP TIPS   TOP TIPS

■ Be versatile in your early development as a coach, it will keep your options broader before you specialise.

■ Remember to consider how other people see you as a coach – is this 'person' someone you like or should you be adapting some aspects?

■ Consider feedback; it helps your own personal development.

■ Learn from other coaches whenever the opportunity arises.

THE PRACTICAL APPLICATION OF COACHING

THE FIRST PART OF THIS CHAPTER WILL LOOK AT THE 'IDEAL' FACILITIES IN WHICH TO TEACH RIDERS AND THEN POINT OUT THAT WHILE CONSIDERATION IS GIVEN TO THE ENVIRONMENT AND HOW IT INFLUENCES YOUR PLANNING, NEVERTHELESS IT'S THE COACH'S ABILITY TO COMMUNICATE AND FACILITATE PRACTICE THAT IS SO ESSENTIAL AND FUNDAMENTAL. THE SECOND PART OF THE CHAPTER WILL LOOK AT LESSON EXERCISES AND PROBLEM-SOLVING, REFLECTION AND MAINTAINING SELF-MOTIVATION.

Facilities

Where you give a riding lesson can affect your *planning*, *development* and *outcomes* quite drastically. A group of riders taught in one situation may be able to develop in a completely different way from a group of riders taught elsewhere. Consider the person who has never ridden anywhere but in an enclosed arena with an artificial surface under constant supervision. Their approach to riding is going to be very different from the rider who has only ridden on the hills, bridlepaths and beaches around their home, and has grown up with horses as a natural part of their upbringing.

Riding facilities have improved dramatically over the last three decades and as equestrian sport continues to enjoy a rise in popularity they are likely to continue to develop, with more and more riders learning and training in a structured environment. The increased awareness of the need for safety at all times has also contributed to the heightened concentration on ensuring that the riders are not challenged beyond their ability.

I believe passionately however that, in riding, either the rider (if old enough – i.e. over eighteen) or the parent/guardian must take some responsibility for the fact that, by its nature, the sport has a large element of risk. No instructor/coach (however competent and experienced they are) can *guarantee* that a rider will never experience some kind of incident, possibly an injury resulting from a fall or from some interaction with a very large animal weighing around half a ton (e.g. being trodden on or kicked).

Lessons in modern, well-maintained arenas.

Your responsibility as a coach is to ensure that, at all times, you have taken every reasonable precaution and you have used clear, identifiable judgement in every situation to safeguard your pupil(s) to the best of your ability. 'Negligence' implies that you have neglected that obligation, in which case you could be held liable. However, if you have not acted in a negligent way, but the unpredictability of the horse created a circumstance beyond your control, then it is an unfortunate accident, for which you could not be held responsible (although someone may try very hard!). Make absolutely sure that in your work as a coach you keep an identifiable record of all the lessons you give and certainly that there is a clear written record made of any incident that occurs involving a horse and rider in your care. Also, be sure to evaluate teaching facilities to ensure that they are fit for purpose and, if you have any concerns, take these into account and tailor your lessons accordingly.

Facilities that you use may include:

• **An enclosed indoor arena with an artificial surface.**
Ensure that you know how the surface reacts when wet/dry or deep. Know whether the school becomes very hot or cold or dusty. Consider the access, viewing area, distractions such as a café at arena side.

• **An outdoor arena with an artificial surface.**
Know whether the surface becomes wet (water lying on it), deep, inconsistent, dry, hard, dusty. Consider the surround – fence, kicking boards, bank, trees. Consider the access, surrounding possible distractions (car park, fields with horses around).

• **A field.**
Consider size, any restraint e.g. corner with hedges, surface (deep, dry, hard, slippery) and any distractions around.

• **Open country when hacking out.**
Consider terrain, other users of the area, traffic and numbers being escorted.

• **Competition venues, including the working-in area.**
Consider other riders using the area; external distractions. If such venues are used for schooling days (e.g. cross-country), it may be prudent to liaise with other groups or individuals using the facilities.

If you are working in your own riding school or private teaching facilities, then you should consider having a risk assessment in place of the possible hazards that the facility might produce. For example, if your indoor school borders a main road with heavy traffic thundering by, the chances are that your school horses are well used to the noise. However, a horse coming for a first lesson with a private client may find the noise and vehicle presence quite difficult to get used to. You would need to address this with a policy whereby you might lunge the horse first without the rider. You may start in walk and trot, away from the noisiest part of the school, and you might book the rider on a Sunday or an evening first, when the school is quieter, to allow the horse to get used to the environment before coming at a noisier time. You have then used judgement in reducing the risk of the traffic presence that you cannot actually eradicate.

When teaching novice riders, a safe, enclosed area is a definite advantage, but this does not mean that, without this facility, people cannot learn to ride. Consider the swimmer learning to swim in a small pool with only a few people around and a water depth of less than 4 feet. Consider that same person learning to swim in the sea with a steep, shelving beach so that they quickly get out of their depth. The second situation would be more challenging, but the good teacher would still facilitate the learning.

If you are a freelance coach, working at different venues, you can't have a set risk assessment in place, but you must learn to:

• Look at every facility in which you are going to coach.

• Consider size, surface, enclosure, changes in footing, access, outside influence and noise (permanent and intermittent).

• Consider the number of riders you may have in your control.

• Consider whether you are the only person using the facility.

• Consider what 'props' you might need (poles, jump stands, cones, etc.), where these might be stored and how accessible they would be.

• Consider what help (if any) there might be if there was an emergency.

• Consider the availability of a telephone (mobile or land line).

• Consider facilities such as a loo, warm dry area where a rider (or supporter) could relax and perhaps make a warm drink, or get dry again after being wet or cold.

• Consider possible circumstances that might change the safety of the facility. (Surface is fine when dry but is deep and unrideable when wet.)

• Ensure that the surface(s) on which you teach are maintained in as good condition as possible. This must include removal of droppings, regular levelling, harrowing and particular attention to the track, which takes the most wear.

• Also remember that neglect of the surface could constitute an abandonment of the 'duty of care' of the proprietor to provide a safe working environment for both you (the coach) and the client (public). You would be seen as having complicity in the case of an incident brought about through neglect of the surface.

• Remember that any equipment such as poles, jump stands, plastic blocks, cones or any other 'props' are your responsibility and you must 'manage' them in a competent and organised way. Always ensure that equipment you use is in good, well-maintained condition and that it is used in a safe way.

Problem-solving and exercises for lessons

There is no substitute for experience and without doubt, as your years of 'doing it' increase, you should become a more practised and competent coach. I believe that one of the most effective way of developing is to observe and learn from other coaches. In this respect, I am often asked, 'What would you do if…?', or 'What would you do in a situation where…happened?' In the following section I hope that some of the exercises and suggestions I offer for certain situations may help to expand your own repertoire as a coach.

Establishing aims and solving problems

In my own training of riders I *always* ask them what their aim is 'today'. This may be one of the most important questions you ever ask your rider. Even with a rider you know very well and have taught for a long time, you cannot and should not assume that you know what they are feeling or want to do on any occasion when you meet for training. By asking what their aim is or what they want to work on, you put the responsibility on them to think and make a decision about the direction of the training. Straight away you therefore encourage a *joint responsibility* to the work; the rider has been involved in the decision-making and is then more likely to commit to the effort required for improvement.

A problem may be seen as a situation difficult to resolve or manage. The successful outcome of a problem is therefore a solution. Is there a general plan that could be applied to all 'problems' to arrive at a solution? In the broadest terms the answer is probably 'yes'.

Of course there will be many variables (e.g. individual rider or groups of riders, young horse or older school horse, limited time to arrive at the solution, etc. etc.). Of course, the ideal and the easiest approach is to avoid creating a problem in the first place!

Avoiding problems

Pre-planning
• Consider the facilities in which you will be coaching.

• Consider the number of riders you will be coaching.

• Consider the time you will have allocated for the session (it will help you to decide what work you can realistically cover in the time).

• Consider the existing knowledge you have of the rider(s). (Have you met or taught them before, or is this the first time?)

• Consider any other factors that might affect the session (e.g. time of day, weather conditions).

Within the session
• Ensure a period of introduction (as important for you to find out about the rider(s) as for them to feel at ease with you).

• *Questions* will tell you a great deal at this stage.

• Discuss with the rider(s) the *agreed plan*.

• Develop the initial stages of the lesson (warming up horse and rider) and *assess* and *evaluate* at this stage and throughout the whole training.

• *Discuss* and *question* at appropriate stages throughout the session so that the plan can be flexible and adjusted to meet the needs of the rider(s).

• Ensure that each rider takes as much *responsibility* as they are capable of in the lesson.

• *Encourage, praise, support* and *challenge* the rider(s).

• Constant awareness of each rider's state of confidence and competence will ensure smooth progression of the plan.

• Ensure that you finish 'on a good note', maintaining the confidence of the rider(s).

• The session should *stimulate* and *motivate*.

Post-session
• Always 'warm down' or 'cool down' your horses and riders. This is important both physically and mentally after effort and exertion; it is important that pupils are able to 'wind down' and *reflect*.

• Always ensure that you have questioned your rider(s) to confirm their understanding of the work you have covered.

• Rider(s) may feel challenged by the session but should not go away overwhelmed by what you have worked on.

• Give your rider(s) a focus to go home with – some amount of 'homework' helps the ongoing progression of their work and provides a link between the work covered 'today' and the next lesson.

Exercises for lessons

Every instructor/coach has their own 'dictionary' of exercises that they use on a regular basis for training horses and riders at every level. I think of teaching riding as a bit like having a good command of another language. The greater your vocabulary the more versatile you are in speaking the language. Your command of the grammar allows you to actually string the words together in an articulate way.

I make no apology for saying again that a good coach learns much from watching other good coaches. Inevitably one increases one's own repertoire of exercises and ways of working horses and riders by picking up plans from others. However, you still have to know when to use the exercises and for how long. You still have to know when an exercise is working and when you need to change it slightly for 'that horse' or 'this rider'. That is when your skill as a coach begins to shine through, when your pupils begin to excel as a result of your work with them. You cannot 'just copy' another instructor/coach.

As a coach you must develop your own blend of:
✦   Skill and technical knowledge.
✦   Empathy, enthusiasm and commitment to all your pupils.
✦   Understanding.
✦   Patience.
✦   Drive.
✦   Awareness and judgement.
✦   Tact, fairness and authority.

Finally, I believe that while there are many, many good coaches there are only a few really *great* coaches. And the ingredients that make the difference, are, I think *personality* and *passion*.

Referring back to the analogy of grammar requirements for learning a language, I think the fundamental 'grammatical' requirements in the coaching of horses and riders are:

For the rider: a balanced, effective, supple independent position.

For the horse: reference to the German 'Scales of Training' – Relaxation, Rhythm, Suppleness, Connection, Impulsion, Straightness and Collection, with balance and forward movement being the common denominator that tie all these criteria together.

I have previously stated that this is not fundamentally a book about training horses or riders as such; it is a book about improving your coaching skills. However, the following are a few exercises that I use frequently which you can use to 'try out' your improved skills. The exercises have brief explanations about how to ride them and in what ways they benefit horse and rider. Some of the explanations are inherent in the description of the exercises; where necessary, further explanation is given.

(It is always important that both horses and riders loosen up and warm up progressively before any actual work is started. Riders should be encouraged to use some suppling exercises and some form of stretching before they mount.)

Exercise 1

Exercise 1

- Ride the horse in trot on both reins (rising) circling (20 m) at the A and C ends of the school to begin the suppling process.

- Encourage the horse to stretch forward to the contact and, if he is tense, encourage him to lower his neck and work in a long stretch over his back to the contact.

• Rider's position should be balanced and in harmony with the horse. Rider should be supple and elastic through arms and wrists, knees and ankles.

Exercise 2

• Turn across the school and make transitions over the centre line. (Walk transitions first then progressively to halt and then directly halt to trot and trot to halt.)

• Work on the suppleness and balance in the turn (both reins).

• Work on the rhythm in the gait before and after the transitions.

• Work on the rider's balance through the turns and the ability of the rider to bring the transition from the hind legs to the contact.

• Work on the rider's 'feel' of the hind legs through the transitions, especially into halt.

Exercise 3

• Work around the school going large; make small changes in the trot by bringing the horse more onto the hind legs with half-halts, then riding the trot into bigger, more ground-covering strides while trying to keep the same rhythm and tempo.

• Work to improve the rider's balance in the shortening and lengthening of the trot and their ability to feel the rhythm and activity in the trot.

• Some lengthening on the diagonal would be a natural progression from this exercise.

Exercise 4

• Decreasing progressively from a 20 m circle towards 15 m and then 10 m, in walk, trot and canter according to horse's/rider's ability, staying aware of the 'straightness' of the horse (i.e. hind legs tracking the front legs).

• The rider to stay aware of their balance and ability to follow the bend of the horse.

• The rider to feel the balance and bend through the body and not increase the neck bend only.

• Then increase the size of the circle either by spiralling out 'straight' or by leg-yielding out. In the latter case the rider must stay aware of the forwardness and sideways movement and not increase the neck bend (which might cause the horse to 'escape' through the outside shoulder).

Exercise 5

• Canter a 20 m circle on the centre of the school (E or B). Be aware of the control of the outside shoulder on the circle. Focus on the horse's straightness on the circle.

• Make transitions to trot on the circle at E or B and then back to canter again at the next marker. Alternatively, shorten the canter for half the circle and lengthen on the other half of the circle.

  ✦ *Both these exercises improve the feel and timing of the rider.*

  ✦ *The transitions improve the horse's response to the aids both within the gait and from one gait to the other (trot, canter, trot).*

Exercise 6

• Going large around the school in trot.

• In each corner ride forward to walk and ride the corner in walk then retake trot after the corner.

• The corners on the short side come up quickly so the rider must be focused on preparing for the transitions.

  ✦ *This exercise improves the preparation and timing of the rider's aids.*

  ✦ *This exercise improves the suppleness and engagement of the horse's hind legs and his balance and obedience in the corners.*

Exercise 7

Exercise 7

- Decrease the circle from 20 m progressively to 10 m in trot.

- Make a transition to walk and continue on the same rein while preparing to make a small half-circle outwards to return to the 20 m circle on the other rein.

- On reaching the new large circle, make a transition to canter directly from walk.

- Proceed in canter on the new rein and then repeat the exercise as appropriate.

    ✦ *This exercise improves suppleness of the horse and responsiveness to the aids.*

    ✦ *For the rider this exercise improves feel and timing of aid application.*

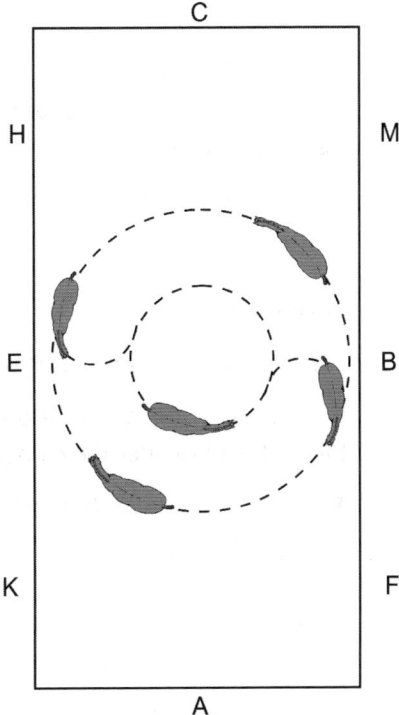

Exercise 7 – decreasing circle.

Exercise 8

Exercise 8

• Going large around the school, make a transition to walk and then halt at A or C.

• Taking a slightly inside track, make a turn on the forehand to change the rein.

• Before reaching the next corner, make a transition from walk to canter and proceed in canter.

• At the half marker on the next long side make a transition to trot and then walk at the next quarter marker.

• Repeat the turn on the forehand just to the inside of A or C and repeat the exercise.

   ✦   *This exercise improves the rider's timing, feel and co-ordination of aids.*

   ✦   *The horse improves in response to the aids and develops some suppleness from the turns on the forehand.*

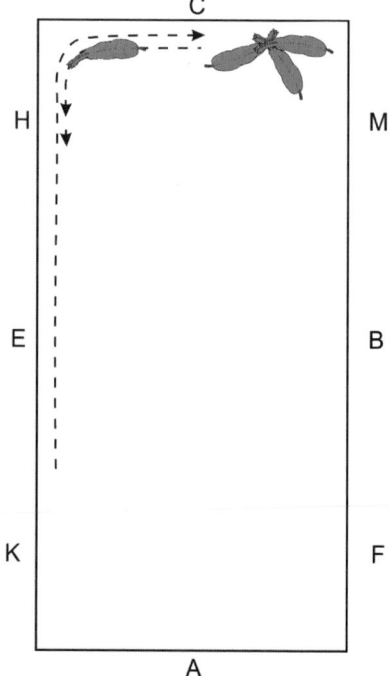

Exercise 8 – turn on the forehand.

Exercise 9

Exercise 9

● Working in trot (or canter to make the exercise more challenging), make a 20 m circle at E or B.

● On crossing the centre line, make a transition down (to walk or trot depending on the original gait).

● Immediately make a 10 m circle to the outside of the original large circle (see diagram), in effect changing the rein into the small circle.

● On completing the small circle, change the rein back onto the original 20 m circle.

● Make these transitions and small circles every time the centre line is crossed.

✦ *This exercise improves the horse's suppleness.*

✦ *For the rider, it improves feel and aid co-ordination. This exercise can be adapted to be as demanding as you want by making the transitions from walk to canter and in due course involve simple changes and flying changes.*

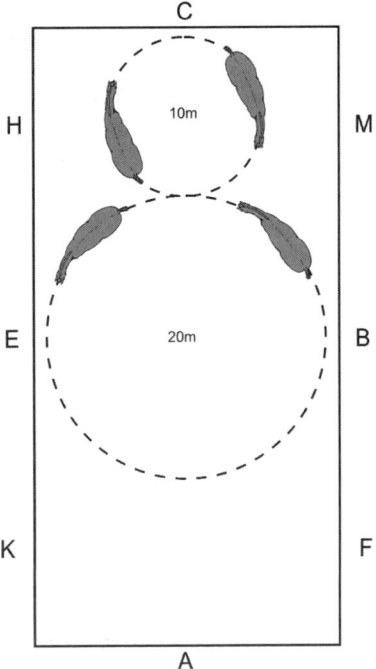

Exercise 9 – circling to the outside.

Exercise 10

Exercise 10

● Ride a serpentine of three or four loops in trot.

● Over the centre line, make a transition to walk for two or three steps and retake trot.

✦ *This exercise improves the suppleness of the horse.*

✦ *It improves the timing and co-ordination of the aids and the ability of the rider to make accurate loops and transitions.*

This exercise could be ridden in canter with changes of lead through trot, simple changes or flying changes.

All these exercises are only patterns in the school in a variety of gaits. However, ridden well, with thought and preparation, they will develop the athleticism of the horse and improve his basic gaits. They have the potential for improving the rider's preparation, awareness and timing of aid applications. They should improve feel and co-ordination in the rider. Their benefit will only be felt with correct execution and recognition of the effect they are having.

The exercises should be most useful to you in your work and, through using them, you should improve your recognition of where and when they help specific horses or riders.

I have only included exercises on the flat. There are many excellent books available that will offer exercises for more work on the flat and for jumping. I will leave you to seek them out and use the range of exercises available to develop your repertoire. This leads me very easily into the subject of *reflection* and maintaining *self-motivation*.

Reflection

As a coach it is important that you constantly consider what you have done in your work and encourage your pupils to regularly assess their own past performances both in training and competition.

Reflection gives you a strong platform from which to project your further training. It also encourages your pupils to consider their whole performance, whether a training session or a competitive outing, and review the strengths and weaknesses of the activity. If this review takes place as a matter of course between you and your pupils, it gives both parties a wealth of information that you can use in further training.

It is important to learn to reflect constructively. Often people focus only on the negative aspects of what they have done (both in training and competition). It is your role to help your pupils reflect in such a way that both positives and negatives are identified, so that in the future the positives are maintained and built upon, while the negatives are considered with a view to reducing or eradicating them.

Reflection can and will occur immediately after performance, but it should also be ongoing. At the beginning of a training session it is likely that there will be a moment of reflection on the previous lesson; this is valuable and may refresh the memory of the last work and assist *planning* for the new session.

Regarding self-reflection, for my own benefit as a coach, I keep a work diary of all the lessons I teach. This enables me to look back at the work I covered with a rider (which may be four to six weeks ago, or even longer). I can then recall the work we covered and refresh my memory of the issues that arose in the lesson. It is important for the rider to feel that you do remember their particular issues and you are not just going through a stereotyped lesson with little regard for their individual needs.

Reflection ensures ongoing *assessment, evaluation* and *planning*.

Maintaining self-motivation

- What drives you to be a better coach?

- What stimulates you to improve yourself?

- When do you feel excited or challenged by your profession as a coach?

It is human nature to feel motivated sometimes and not at others. We have discussed the circumstances that will motivate your pupils and in many instances they can be the same motivators for you as well. As a professional you are earning a living by your coaching and therefore you have some responsibility to your pupils to provide them with interesting, lively, well-planned training sessions. The more experienced you become the easier it is to do this even if you are not feeling totally self-motivated on any occasion. You cannot get away with it for long, however, and I believe that our profession is dependent on coaching coming 'from the heart'. Our work is vocational; we chose it for the 'love of it'; for the satisfaction that we get from working with the horse and for being able to transfer the huge love and enjoyment we get from the horse to other people (our pupils) – this is the reward for the profession we chose. For myself, if the day comes when I don't have a desire to be better today as a coach than I was yesterday then I shall give up coaching.

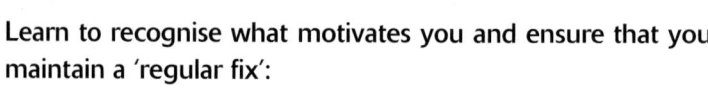

Learn to recognise what motivates you and ensure that you maintain a 'regular fix':

✦ It may be that you need to compete yourself.

✦ Maybe you need to go to competitions of a high standard and feel inspired to raise your pupils to that level.

✦ Taking training yourself may be a motivator.

✦ Attending courses, conventions and seminars may be motivating.

✦ Mixing with other coaches and sharing experiences is usually motivating.

SUMMARY

CHAPTER 12

■ **FACILITIES AFFECT WHAT YOU TEACH AND HOW YOU PLAN AND PROGRESS.**

■ **CONSIDER PROBLEMS AS HAVING A SURMOUNTABLE SOLUTION.**

■ **AVOID PROBLEMS BY GOOD PREPARATION AND PLANNING.**

■ **EXERCISES ARE A FRAMEWORK FOR DEVELOPMENT.**

■ **REFLECTION IS ESSENTIAL FOR MAINTAINING GOOD FORWARD PLANNING.**

■ **SELF-MOTIVATION IS ESSENTIAL FOR THE CONTINUED BENEFIT OF YOUR PUPILS.**

TOP TIPS TOP TIPS TOP TIPS TOP TIPS

■ Learn to be versatile – don't see a lack of facilities as a barrier to your ability to coach riders.

■ Be positive about dealing with problems, there is always a solution.

■ Plan exercises that suit horses and riders.

■ Use reflection to consider the strengths and weaknesses of your work.

■ When you no longer feel driven to be a better coach it may be time to take a holiday.

UNDERSTANDING YOUR SPORT

AS A PROFESSIONAL COACH EARNING ANY KIND OF LIVING FROM EQUESTRIAN SPORT IT IS ESSENTIAL THAT YOU HAVE A WORKING KNOWLEDGE OF HOW OUR SPORT RUNS AND THEREFORE WHAT OPPORTUNITIES EXIST – IN PARTICULAR FOR COMPETITIVE RIDERS AND THUS FOR THEIR COACHES. IT IS INEVITABLE THAT, IN YOUR WORKING LIFE, YOU WILL HAVE SOME INPUT IN COACHING 'COMPETITION RIDERS', EVEN IF THIS STARTS WITH AN 'IN-HOUSE' TRAINING COMPETITION IN THE RIDING SCHOOL WHERE YOU ARE AN 'INSTRUCTOR'.

The British Equestrian Federation and member bodies

The British Equestrian Federation (BEF) is the governing body for equestrian sports in the United Kingdom. The BEF is affiliated to the Federation Equestre Internationale (FEI) – the international governing body of most major equestrian sports except racing – and as such works on behalf of the UK on issues of policy, the international events calendar and the overseas training of British international judges (and vets, course designers and stewards).

In the UK the BEF is the umbrella organisation representing sixteen independent member bodies (see below) to organisations such as the British Olympic Association (BOA), The Sport Aid Foundation and the Central Council for Physical Recreation (CCPR). The BEF is responsible for distributing government funding to its member bodies. Funding is available to equestrian sports through Sport England, UK Sport, the Lottery funded World Class Performance Programme and from Sport Scotland for the Scottish Equestrian Association (SEA).

The BEF, in association with the British Horse Racing Board (BHRB) and the Thoroughbred Breeders' Association (TBA), forms the British Horse Industry Confederation (BHIC) which is a vital link with government to lobby on horse-related issues. The sixteen member bodies of the BEF are:

British Dressage (BD): www.britishdressage.co.uk

British Eventing (BE): www.britisheventing.com

British Show Jumping Association (BSJA): www.bsja.co.uk

British Horse Society (BHS): www.bhs.org.uk

The Pony Club (PC): www.pcuk.org

British Equestrian Vaulting: www.vaulting.org.uk

British Horse Driving Trials Association: www.horsedrivingtrials.co.uk

British Reining (BR): www.britishreining.co.uk

Endurance GB: www.endurancegb.co.uk

Association of British Riding Schools (ABRS): www.abrs-info.org

British Equestrian Trade Association (BETA): www.beta-uk.org

Scottish Equestrian Association (SEA): www.s-e-a.org.uk

Riding for the Disabled Association (RDA): www.rda.org.uk

British Horseball Association (BHA): www.horseball.org.uk

Mounted Games Association of GB: www.mgagb.co.uk

UK Polocrosse Association: www.polocrosse.org.uk

Of the sports administered by the associations listed, endurance riding, vaulting and reining are now included in Equestrian World Championship competitions and reining is an Olympic discipline. Paralympic dressage is now an integral part of the FEI and is managed by the IPEC (International Paralympic Equestrian Committee).

While there are specialist coaches for these disciplines, unless you are one of them it is very likely that you are involved in some aspect of coaching in the main three Olympic disciplines: show jumping, eventing and dressage.

British Dressage

British Dressage, the governing body for dressage and paralympic dressage in the UK, promotes the interests of members interested in that discipline. It manages the organisation of dressage as a sport through affiliated competitions throughout the country. It has an expanding membership and is especially developing the interests of youngsters coming into the sport through the British Young Riders' Dressage Scheme (BYRDS). Regional training is available through a network of committees and development officers who organise activities in all areas of the UK. Regional training leads into national training at all levels, from which élite riders are recognised and selected for further training towards British international dressage teams.

British Eventing

British Eventing is the governing body for eventing in the UK. Eventing, an all-round test of horsemanship (dressage, riding across country and show jumping), is one of Great Britain's most successful sports in terms of medals won at major championships (Olympic, World or European level). Along with dressage and show jumping, it is one of the few sports in which men and women compete on equal terms. It is also an excellent spectator sport (Badminton International three-day event has one of the largest attendance figures in the world for a one-day sporting spectacle, i.e. cross-country day).

British Eventing provides opportunities for all ages and abilities both in competition and through regional training in the UK. The UK is regarded by many other countries as the 'Mecca' of eventing and as such Australian, New Zealand, German and Scandinavian riders are attracted to come here and take advantage of the wide range of training and competitive opportunities available throughout a large part of every year.

British Show Jumping Association

The British Show Jumping Association is the governing body for show jumping in the UK. It aims to improve standards of show jumping at all levels from novice to top class international. Affiliated competitions are run throughout the BSJA's area of jurisdiction on most days of every week. There are three flagship shows of the year: the Royal International Horse Show in the summer and the Christmas Show at Olympia in December are popular with riders from home and abroad, and the evergreen Horse of the Year Show provides an autumn extravaganza of show jumping championships as well as a large range of other equestrian activities such as mounted games and showing classes.

Competing and coaching

As a rider it is very likely that you yourself will be a member of one or more of the bodies mentioned.

> • *Are you a competitor?*
>
> • *What does competition teach you (and therefore how does this impact on the pupils you teach)?*
>
> • *How familiar are you with your discipline's rules and regulations?*
>
> • *In what practical way can you encourage your pupils to develop a responsibility towards rules for the sports they are choosing to follow?*

Riders gain a huge amount of experience by competing actively. Some of these riders then develop into outstanding coaches. The idea that the expertise accumulated as a competitor is then transferred to others hoping to progress in the sport is to be encouraged. The key to this is effective *communication*, an attribute that has been emphasised throughout this book. In practice, some people who may not have had a high level of competitive experience may have excellent communication skills and they may be better 'teachers' than someone who has all the experience but no patience or ability to recognise that they must be able to *communicate* to transfer that experience to less able pupils. Although it is not necessarily the case that the ability to 'do' and the ability to 'teach' are mutually exclusive, they *are* different skills. Studying for coaching qualifications can develop communication skills and help people who are primarily 'practitioners' become effective teachers as well.

The British Horse Society and its role in instruction

The British Horse Society is the largest, most influential equestrian charity in the UK, its large membership reflecting the commitment of many to equine welfare and aspects such as safety, access and rights of way. While it is a member body of the BEF, the BHS is given special consideration here because, in addition to the charitable objectives mentioned, it has a strong association with riding instruction and thus with the career development and employment of equestrian teaching professionals.

One aspect of this is its affiliated group of Riding Clubs throughout the UK that offer recreational riding, training and club-level competition to the amateur horse owner and enthusiast. These clubs (and the Pony Club) provide opportunities for those with teaching ambitions to develop their own riding skills and, in due course, to offer their professional services as instructors.

The British Horse Society also operates a system for the approval and registering of riding schools and livery yards, which encourages a good standard of horse care and, in the case of riding schools, good levels of instruction. Again, this has twofold benefits for teaching professionals in that it provides a good level of instruction when they themselves are at the 'learning' stage, and a potential source of income when they have qualified and are teaching.

This brings us to the third contribution that the BHS makes in the field of instruction. The Society has long been recognised as having a world-renowned system of progressive qualifications that ensures competence in riding, horse management and teaching skills (instruction). Qualified instructors are listed in a *Register of Instructors* but, to maintain their status on this register, they are required to hold a current first aid certificate, to have attended training in aspects of child protection, to maintain their own personal development and to have active third party insurance cover.

At this point, some mention should be made of The Association of British Riding Schools – in essence, a trade association – which also operates an approval and affiliation system for member schools and runs a system of instructor qualifications, the latter being more directed at the instructor who will work in a commercial riding school with the emphasis on educating groups of weekly riders and providing a safe but fun learning environment. Many riding schools are both affiliated to the BHS and members of the ABRS.

Other training and coaching qualifications and initiatives

International Group for Equestrian Qualifications

As a qualified instructor it is possible to apply to hold an International Trainer's Passport through the International Group for Equestrian Qualifications (IGEQ: www.igeq.org). The International Group is an independent body that involves a membership of over thirty countries world-wide. The aim of the IGEQ is to ensure a harmonisation of qualifications in each member country, to share good practice between countries and to facilitate the development of qualifications in nations as yet not as forward in that respect as the UK.

United Kingdom Coaching Certificate

The United Kingdom Coaching Certificate (UKCC) is an initiative to endorse coach education programmes and enhance coaching practice across all sports in the UK. It is aimed at supporting the development of coaching as a more fully recognised profession and it is helping sport (in general) to consider its existing practice and develop programmes from existing expertise.

In the UK, the British Equestrian Federation has established a Coaching Development Action Team that has worked tirelessly to set up a UKCC in Equestrian Sport that will serve all equestrian disciplines. The certificate is expected to be generic at Levels 1 and 2 and then from Level 3 there will be an essential specialisation of coaches in individual disciplines (e.g. dressage or show jumping specialist coach from level 3).

The UKCC is an endorsement of sport-specific coach education qualifications that are aligned to an agreed national framework. By creating a recognised standard of coach education nationally, the

UKCC will make it easier to identify a proficient coach in any sport at any level and will contribute greatly to the professionalism of coaching.

The UKCC will ensure that all sports are delivering the best athlete-centred coaching possible and that, in due course, they will reap the increased rewards of this both in terms of competition success and in the recreational enjoyment of sport.

Long term athlete development

In Great Britain the government is looking at sport and physical education in general as areas where significant improvements can be made to health, social inclusion, educational attainment and national pride.

Everyone, whether sports coach, school teacher, parent or player has a responsibility to encourage youngsters today to embrace good health through regular exercise and sport.

The LTAD model (which I will outline briefly here) has been pioneered by the worldwide expert on the subject, Istvan Balyi. Istvan has travelled extensively throughout the sporting world to produce this plan, which is a total philosophy for sports development and is likely to prove a real tool for change in the future. All sports are being encouraged to develop it within their own specialist area.

LTAD outlines a staged approach to appropriate training, competition and recovery programming in relation to the developmental age of an individual. LTAD is intended to produce a long-term approach to maximising individual potential and involvement in sport.

In relation to coaching, LTAD highlights the importance of having high-quality coaches working with and understanding the development of children and young people as they embark on their sporting journey. While aiming to develop the sports person to the highest level, the LTAD framework will also encourage and support all participants to stay involved in sport at every level to fulfil their own personal potential, aims or aspirations. It will provide an opportunity for a lifelong involvement in sport with all the benefits to health and well-being that this can promote.

LTAD defines the best environment or activity for (in equestrian sport) riders, drivers or vaulters to develop. It applies to recreational as well as competitive athletes (riders, drivers or vaulters). The plan considers each age group and provides common stages of development through an equestrian lifespan or career. It offers advice to the athlete's parents, family, coach, etc., intended to best support their development in equestrian sport and extend their personal satisfaction and enjoyment of the sport.

The BEF has been working across equestrian disciplines to finalise an LTAD framework for equestrian sport and specific disciplines will be taking this forward for the future. The BEF believes that a similar framework could evolve to consider the equine athlete specifically and thus in conjunction with LTAD is the emerging concept that, in our sport, LTED (Long Term Equine Development) is important to consider.

General information on this topic is available from SCUK LTAD (Sports Coach UK).

Summary of the LTAD framework for equestrianism

In brief, the LTAD framework for equestrianism encompasses three stages of development.

Stage 1: Learning to ride and train

FUNdamentals. The philosophy is about safety – enjoyment – learning.

Rider age: target age group 6 to 12 (but may be any age depending on when the sport is taken up).

This stage is about the 'developing rider'.

The rider is working to achieve basic riding skills – balance – confidence – feel – harmony – empathy – interest – fun – control of the equine – values and respect for the horse.

The rider is developing a well-structured approach to riding as an all-year activity and sport. If a child, then ideally the child is involved in several other sports and through a multi-discipline approach is developing core skills of technical elements (e.g. eye to hand co-ordination, core stability) that will serve them in any sport.

Stage 2: Riding and training to compete

Philosophy: Safety – Satisfaction – Learning.

Rider age: 12 to 16 (target ages).

This stage is for developing the 'competent rider'.

The rider is developing in all aspects of horsemanship – understanding the equine – equine physiology – equine development – horsemastership.

The rider is developing training programmes, balanced development in all aspects of the sport and evolving competitive skill.

Stage 3: Riding and training to win

Philosophy: safety – satisfaction – performance.

Rider age: 16 to 21 and 21 to 35+

This stage is about the 'complete rider and competitor'.

At age 16 to 21, the rider is developing event-specific skills – equine training skill – competition preparation – self-discipline.

At age 21 to 35+, the rider is developing – event expertise – competition expertise – equine training expertise.

There will be multiple periods of emphasis on training and competition, and much individual focus.

The intention is to produce a highly focused individual, aiming to maximise their peak performance, with the ability to educate, train and prepare the horse for competition.

Long term athlete development provides an exciting and innovative framework which is likely to readjust the way any individual considers sport and enables them to step into a structure which will support them at whatever level they choose to be involved.

SUMMARY

CHAPTER 13

■ **FOR A COACH, A CLEAR UNDERSTANDING OF HOW OUR SPORT OPERATES IS ESSENTIAL.**

■ **A WORKING UNDERSTANDING OF THE EQUESTRIAN DISCIPLINES THAT UNDERPIN THE RUNNING OF EQUESTRIAN SPORT IS ALSO NECESSARY.**

■ **QUALIFICATIONS MAY CONFIRM THE STANDING YOU ACHIEVE IN THE SPORT AND WILL GIVE A RECOGNISED 'BENCHMARK' OF YOUR LEVEL.**

■ **UKCC AND LTAD REFLECT THE UK'S COMMITMENT TO SPORT AS AN IMPORTANT PART OF A YOUNG PERSON'S DEVELOPMENT AND LIFESTYLE.**

TOP TIPS TOP TIPS TOP TIPS TOP TIPS

■ Stay in touch and up to date with what is going on in your own equestrian sport(s).

■ Understand that progress in our sport is often linked to developments in other sports.

■ As a coach, never miss an opportunity to learn from what other coaches in other sports are doing.

■ Good practice in coaching is evident across all sports.

INDEX